CRUX

CRUX

Radical Philosophy and the Scandal of the Cross

Joseph D. Kuzma

CASCADE *Books* • Eugene, Oregon

CRUX
Radical Philosophy and the Scandal of the Cross

Copyright © 2025 Joseph D. Kuzma. All rights reserved. Except for brief quotations in critical publications or reviews, no part of this book may be reproduced in any manner without prior written permission from the publisher. Write: Permissions, Wipf and Stock Publishers, 199 W. 8th Ave., Suite 3, Eugene, OR 97401.

Cascade Books
An Imprint of Wipf and Stock Publishers
199 W. 8th Ave., Suite 3
Eugene, OR 97401

www.wipfandstock.com

PAPERBACK ISBN: 979-8-3852-5001-1
HARDCOVER ISBN: 979-8-3852-5002-8
EBOOK ISBN: 979-8-3852-5003-5

Cataloguing-in-Publication data:

Names: Kuzma, Joseph D., author.
Title: CRUX : radical philosophy and the scandal of the cross / Joseph D. Kuzma.
Description: Eugene, OR : Cascade Books, 2025 | Includes bibliographical references and index.
Identifiers: ISBN 979-8-3852-5001-1 (paperback) | ISBN 979-8-3852-5002-8 (hardcover) | ISBN 979-8-3852-5003-5 (ebook)
Subjects: LCSH: Faith. | Christianity and culture. | Theology. | Cosmology.
Classification: BT19 .K89 2025 (paperback) | BT19 (ebook)

VERSION NUMBER 11/19/25

Scripture quotations are from the New Revised Standard Version Bible: Catholic Edition, copyright © 1993 National Council of the Churches of Christ in the United States of America. Used by permission. All rights reserved worldwide.

Contents

Introduction: The Violation of Everyday Life | 1
Chapter One: Love's Impossible Gift: Lacan | 6
Chapter Two: Faith Against Itself: Žižek | 26
Chapter Three: The Unbearable Spectacle: Girard | 45
Chapter Four: Breaking the Void: Badiou | 61
Chapter Five: Already After the End: Agamben | 80
Conclusion: Eating God (At the End of Time) | 99

Endnotes | 115
Suggested Reading | 119
Bibliography | 127

Introduction

The Violation of Everyday Life

THOUGH I WAS BAPTIZED as an infant, I fell in love with philosophy before I fell in love with Jesus.

It wasn't just philosophy, though. It was a certain kind of philosophy—the kind that whispered enigmas rather than delivered answers, the kind that kept its secrets just out of reach. By the time I was deep into my PhD studies in the UK, I had developed an insatiable hunger for the esoteric, the aporetic, the obscure. Maurice Blanchot was just an entry point; from there, I chased everything strange and conceptually destabilizing. Paul Celan's near-impenetrable poetry, Jabès's meditations on absence, Bataille's transgressive mysticism. Psychoanalytic thought, too, in its densest, most labyrinthine forms: Abraham and Torok on cryptic mourning, Lacan's endlessly deferred meaning. Obviously, Deleuze and Guattari. Avant-garde cinema, experimental literature, everything eccentric, everything impenetrable. If it was difficult, disturbing, or resistant to immediate understanding, I was obsessed with it.

On certain nights, I would stay up until dawn—dizzy with theory, hollowed out by caffeine and exhaustion—devouring Thomas Bernhard or Georges Perec, or maybe the experimental, little-read British novelist Ann Quin, whose prose felt like a series of small implosions. Sometimes, when I needed something even more fractured, I'd return to Guyotat's *Eden, Eden, Eden*, which reads like someone took the very structure of language and cracked it open with a rock. It was an addiction, really. A hunger to stand at the edge of meaning and peer over the side.

And then, just like that, the PhD was over.

I returned to the States, armed with a freshly minted doctorate, and absolutely no plan. The immediate reality was stark: no job, no steady income, no immediate prospects. I went from parsing Lacan to filing for food stamps, from reading esoteric French theorists to filling out adjunct job applications that, more often than not, went unanswered.

༄

One Saturday evening—somehow—I wound up in a place I least expected to find myself: standing next to my mom and dad, of all people, at a Catholic Mass.

It was supposed to be temporary, an act of politeness, maybe even nostalgia. A kind of existential placeholder while I figured out the next move. But looking back, I see that something was already working on me in ways I couldn't yet understand.

Though I had technically been Catholic from birth, I could have summed up everything I knew about the faith in two or three sentences. Here I was—twenty-nine years old, fresh out of grad school, having spent years circling the outer edges of meaning—suddenly confronted with a reality that had been there all along. A reality I had completely ignored.

But it wasn't doctrine that struck me first. It wasn't theology, or apologetics, or some intellectual realization about the coherence of Catholic teaching. In those first few visits to Mass, I didn't understand transubstantiation, or ecclesiology, or sacramental theology. And I wasn't trying to.

What struck me—what lodged itself in my chest, sharp and immovable—was simply how otherworldly it all felt.

The sheer weirdness of it.

Here we were, inside a relatively unremarkable parish church—nothing grand or ancient, just brick walls and fluorescent lights—while outside, the world continued as if none of this was

INTRODUCTION

happening. I remember hearing traffic rush by, the faint sound of car horns in the distance, the occasional murmur of conversation outside. Normal life, proceeding as usual.

And yet, inside—something completely other.

I watched as people knelt on command, as they recited prayers I barely remembered. I listened as the priest spoke ancient words over bread and wine. And at the center of it all—looming above the altar—was a massive crucifix: a man being tortured to death.

It was almost offensive.

It violated something—decorum, politeness, normalcy. Even sanity.

I had spent years chasing the extreme, the experimental, the destabilizing—and yet nothing in all my avant-garde reading, nothing in all my attempts to deconstruct meaning, had prepared me for this. For the sheer violence of this image.

A broken body. Nails driven through flesh. Blood streaming from a mangled face.

The entire faith seemed to hinge on this moment, this scene of total rupture, a spectacle of abandonment and agony.

And yet—somehow—I was drawn to it.

I didn't know why.

Maybe, after all those years of seeking the esoteric, the transgressive, the conceptually impossible, I had finally stumbled upon the one thing that was so strange, so incomprehensible, so utterly offensive to the logic of the world, that I couldn't look away.

The Cross. The thing that should not make sense. The ultimate violation of human reason.

But there it was. And here I was, staring at it—feeling, for the first time in my life, like I was seeing something truly Real.

I had spent my PhD years obsessed with what could not be assimilated into ordinary meaning. And in the Cross, I had found something even more radical than anything I had read. Not just an intellectual problem, but a personal crisis.

And maybe—just maybe—that's where faith begins.

CRUX

This book is not a personal memoir. It is not a faith journey, much less a testimony. It is not an attempt at apologetics or a defense of Christian doctrine. I have no "case" to make, no tidy conclusions to offer.

Rather, this is a book about bearing witness to the radical strangeness of the Cross.

That might sound strange itself—after all, isn't the Cross the single most universal symbol in the world? Recognizable across cultures, across history, affixed to hospital walls, worn around necks, inked into skin? How can something so ubiquitous be strange?

And yet, if we take it seriously—if we allow ourselves to really look at it, unshielded by familiarity—we begin to see that the Cross does not function like other symbols. It does not cohere. It does not resolve.

Instead, it interrupts. It disrupts. It violates the very logic of the world.

It is, in this sense, the anti-symbol—an image that does not bring clarity, but confounds. That does not console, but disturbs. If the Cross offers "meaning," it is the kind of meaning that wounds before it heals, that shatters before it saves.

This book does not aim to "explain" the Cross. For that, I would direct you to Scripture, the catechism, the great theological traditions of the church—all of which offer deep, rich, and inexhaustible accounts of the Passion.

This is a book about something else.

The excess of it all. The impossibility of it all. And, above all, the stark, inescapable reality of it all.

I could have approached this mystery through any number of thinkers—poets, mystics, theologians, artists. But I have chosen these five late-twentieth-century Continental theorists (Lacan, Žižek, Girard, Badiou, and Agamben) because each, in his own way, confronts us with a mode of thought that refuses resolution. Each offers a way of thinking that pushes us toward the limits—of language, of subjectivity, of history, of law, of sacrifice.

Introduction

And whether they intended to or not, each gives us tools to think the Cross anew—not as an abstract religious icon, but as an event: a rupture, a scandal, a paradox so deep that it threatens the very structures we use to make sense of the world.

If you are looking for answers, you will not find them here.

But if you are willing to sit with the disruption, to let it unsettle you, then perhaps—somewhere in the excess, in the impossibility, in the sheer offense of the Cross—you will glimpse something of its unbearable truth.

Chapter One
Love's Impossible Gift
Lacan

JACQUES LACAN WAS A figure of contradictions—both a faithful Freudian and a radical revisionist, both a clinician and a philosopher, both revered and infamously difficult. His lectures were part psychoanalytic theory, part theatrical performance, often punctuated by cryptic remarks, sudden dismissals of students, and strange, poetic formulations that seemed deliberately designed to resist easy comprehension. His writing was even more difficult: dense, punning, full of wordplay and mathematical notations. And yet, despite—or perhaps because of—this obscurity, his influence has been immense.

Lacan's major innovation was his claim that "the unconscious is structured like a language."[1] This was a dramatic departure from Freud, who saw the unconscious primarily in terms of drives, repression, and hidden desires. For Freud, the unconscious was a seething cauldron of instincts pressing for expression. Lacan, however, stripped away the biological foundation of Freud's theory and reframed the unconscious as a network of signifiers—a system of meanings that shape our desires, fantasies, and sense of self. To be human, for Lacan, is to be caught in language, to be spoken by the very system we believe we control.

This was part of a broader intellectual movement in twentieth-century France. Thinkers like Claude Lévi-Strauss were applying structuralism to anthropology, showing how myths and kinship systems functioned like languages, with hidden rules and patterns beneath the surface. Lacan did the same for psychoanalysis. But in doing so, he also transformed it. Freud's ideas had already shocked the world by suggesting that we are not masters of our own minds—that we are driven by unconscious forces beyond our control. Lacan took this even further: not only are we ruled by unconscious forces, but those forces themselves are structured by a vast Symbolic Order—a system of meanings, laws, and prohibitions that we inherit before we are even born.[2]

Imagine a newborn child. Before it even speaks, it is already spoken for—named, placed in a family, slotted into a preexisting social structure. A child is called a boy or a girl, assigned a last name, and absorbed into a world of expectations. This is the Symbolic Order in action—it precedes us, determines the range of possible identities we can assume, and structures our experience of reality. We are always "born into" meaning, never outside of it. This is why Lacan often emphasized that man does not speak, but is spoken by language—we are shaped by signifiers that we never chose.

But if language and meaning define us, what happens when meaning fails? What happens when we reach a rupture in the Symbolic Order, a moment when the structures we rely on collapse? What happens when the scaffolding of our identity is stripped away, leaving us in free fall?

This is where Lacan's thought meets the Cross. The crucifixion of Christ is not merely an event within history; it is a rupture in history, a moment when meaning itself seems to tear open. The cry from the Cross—"My God, my God, why have you forsaken me?" (Matt 27:46)—is not only a cry of suffering. It is a cry that marks the failure of meaning itself, a radical break in the Symbolic Order.

But before we can fully understand what the Cross reveals, we must first explore Lacan's three fundamental concepts—the Imaginary, the Symbolic, and the Real[3]—and how they shape our experience of the world. Only then can we begin to grasp the full force of what is happening in the Passion narrative. To do this, we must slow down, unpack these ideas carefully, and consider their implications before making any theological connections.

Lacan was not a theologian, nor was he particularly sympathetic to religion. And yet, his work provides an extraordinary lens for understanding the scandal, the trauma, and the radical disruption of the Cross. To see why, we must first enter *his* world—a world where identity is fractured, language deceives, and meaning is always precarious.

The Three Orders—Imaginary, Symbolic, and Real

Lacan's psychoanalytic framework is built upon three interwoven dimensions of human experience: the Imaginary, the Symbolic, and the Real. These three orders do not represent separate stages of development or distinct psychological categories but are always at work in shaping how we understand ourselves and the world around us. If we are to grasp Lacan's reading of the subject—and ultimately apply it to the Cross—we must first examine these registers in their own right.

The Imaginary Order is the realm of images, illusions, and identifications. It is where the human subject first forms a sense of self, a process Lacan famously describes in his "mirror stage."[4] Picture an infant, six to eighteen months old, seeing its reflection in a mirror. The child experiences a moment of fascination, an apparent recognition—*That is me!* Yet, at this early stage, the infant's motor skills are uncoordinated, its body is fragmented, its experiences disjointed. In other words, the image in the mirror is a fiction of unity, a coherent and whole version of the self that does not yet exist.

This dynamic of recognition and misrecognition finds perhaps its most profound artistic expression in Velázquez's *Las meninas* (1656). The painting presents a dizzying play of gazes and reflections—the artist appears in the canvas, painting something we cannot see, while a mirror in the background reflects the king and queen, who must be standing where we, the viewers, stand.

The painting enacts precisely what Lacan means by the Imaginary: every attempt to capture the self in an image creates a complex web of illusions, reflections, and misrecognitions. We are always seeing ourselves through mirrors within mirrors.

This moment of primal misrecognition establishes a fundamental structure: the self is always mediated by images—images that are deceptive, idealized, external. Even as adults, we remain trapped in the Imaginary whenever we chase fantasies of wholeness—the perfect career, the perfect relationship, the perfect body. Social media, with its carefully curated self-presentations, is one of the most striking contemporary examples of the Imaginary at work. The online persona we construct is a mirror image, an ideal that gives the illusion of coherence. But it is never quite real, and we are never quite satisfied.

If the Imaginary is about images and identifications, the Symbolic Order is about structure, law, and meaning. It is the realm of language, rules, and social expectations—the world of names, prohibitions, and the unconscious web of signifiers that define our existence. The moment a child enters language, it enters the Symbolic. To say *I* is to situate oneself within a system of meanings that long predate us. We are placed into preexisting narratives—family, nationality, gender, religion—before we even have a choice.

The poet Stéphane Mallarmé understood this perfectly. In his groundbreaking poem "Un coup de dés" (A throw of the dice), words scatter across the page like stars in a constellation, suggesting that meaning itself is a vast network of relations that exceeds any individual intention. We don't simply use language; we are caught in its web, spoken by it as much as we speak it. This is what Lacan means by the Symbolic Order—a structure that determines us even as we imagine we are determining it.

But language is never quite adequate to experience. We have all felt it: an overwhelming emotion that words fail to capture, a traumatic event that resists narration. The Symbolic promises coherence, but it is always incomplete. There is always something missing, something left unsaid. This brings us to the third and most unsettling register: the Real.

The Real is not reality in the ordinary sense, but that which resists symbolization. It is what cannot be put into words, what lies beyond the grasp of language. The Real erupts in moments of trauma, in encounters with death, in anything that shatters our normal categories of understanding. Lars von Trier's film *Breaking the Waves* (1996) captures this encounter with the Real in an almost unbearable way. When Bess, the film's protagonist, realizes the full implications of her sacrifice—that her submission to degradation and death might actually be an act of divine love—we witness someone confronting something that cannot be integrated into any normal framework of meaning. Her fate is both horrifying and transcendent, much like the Cross itself.

Imagine receiving devastating news—someone you love is gone. For a moment, everything stops. The world is the same, yet completely altered. There is no meaning, no framework that makes sense of it. That is the Real. The Romanian poet Paul Celan, writing after surviving the Holocaust, tried to forge a new language adequate to this encounter with the Real. His poems, with their broken syntax and invented compound words, embody the struggle to speak the unspeakable. In *Psalm*, he writes of "No-One" kneading "our" nothing—a perfect expression of how the Real ruptures both language and being.[5]

The Cross, as we will see, is an encounter with the Real par excellence. It is the moment when the Symbolic Order—the entire religious and social framework of meaning—collapses. Christ, who was supposed to be the fulfillment of divine promise, hangs on a tree in humiliation. The Messiah dies. The ultimate signifier of hope—God himself—falls into silence. And yet, in this rupture, something new is revealed.

The Name-of-the-Father and the Crisis of Meaning

At the heart of Lacan's theory of the Symbolic Order is the Name-of-the-Father (*Nom-du-Père*)—a term that signifies more than just the paternal figure. It represents the structuring principle that organizes meaning, imposes limits, and stabilizes the subject's relationship to language and law. The Name-of-the-Father is what prevents chaos; it is what makes the world legible. When it functions properly, the Symbolic Order is maintained, and the subject has a coherent (though always incomplete) sense of self. But what happens when the Name-of-the-Father falters? What happens when the structure of meaning itself begins to collapse?

St. Augustine wrestled with this question in his *Confessions*, though in different terms. His famous line—"You have made us for yourself, O Lord, and our hearts are restless until they rest in you"[6]—suggests that divine authority isn't simply imposed from above but is woven into the very structure of human desire. Yet even Augustine recognized moments when this structure trembles. In book 1 of the *Confessions*, he describes an infant's first attempts at language, seeing in this struggle the fundamental human condition: we are beings who must speak, yet our speech always falls short of what we mean to say.

Lacan suggested that modernity is defined by precisely this kind of crisis.[7] Where previous generations lived under clear structures of authority—religion, monarchy, patriarchy—modernity has witnessed their decline. The "death of God," as proclaimed by Nietzsche, was not simply a theological concern; it marked a fundamental rupture in the Symbolic. Without the Name-of-the-Father acting as the central organizing signifier, subjects find themselves in a state of radical disorientation. Meaning becomes fragmented, and the sense of self is destabilized.

Friedrich Hölderlin, writing at the dawn of this modern crisis, captured it with devastating clarity. In his poem "Patmos," he begins with the line "Near is God / And hard to grasp. / But where danger lies, / Grows also what saves."[8] This is not just poetic flourish—it's a profound insight into what happens when divine authority becomes simultaneously more urgent and more impossible to reach. Later in the same poem, Hölderlin speaks of the Father turning away his face, leaving us to grapple with signs and absence—a poetic anticipation of Lacan's theory of the Name-of-the-Father as structured around an essential lack.

CRUX

The Passion narrative presents precisely such a rupture, but in a way that takes the crisis of meaning to its most radical extreme. Christ, the one who is supposed to be the very embodiment of divine authority—the *Logos*, the Word made flesh—undergoes a moment of absolute abandonment. His cry from the Cross, "My God, my God, why have you forsaken me?," is not simply an expression of suffering. It is a moment in which the foundational structure of divine meaning appears to unravel.

Maurice Blanchot, in *The Writing of the Disaster*, provides perhaps the most penetrating modern meditation on this kind of absence. For Blanchot, true absence isn't simply the opposite of presence—it's something more radical, a force that undoes the very categories we use to make sense of the world. When he writes that "the disaster de-scribes,"[9] he means that certain experiences don't simply fail to find meaning; they actively undo our capacity to create meaning at all. This is precisely what happens on the Cross.

To grasp the full weight of this moment, we must recognize that Christ does not simply feel abandoned—he is abandoned. The Father does not intervene. There is no miraculous rescue. No voice from the heavens. The very name that should guarantee order and coherence is absent. The theological scandal of the Cross is that it presents not just suffering, but the failure of meaning itself. The Symbolic is exposed as lacking, and the structure of divine authority is, for a moment, rendered void.

For Lacan, the Name-of-the-Father does not operate as an actual presence but as a structuring absence. It is not that the father is the law, but rather that the father's function is to symbolize the law. In other words, the father's authority does not come from his personal qualities but from his position within the Symbolic Order. This is why, in psychoanalytic theory, the mere invocation of the father's name can produce effects of discipline and order—even if the father himself is weak, absent, or dead.

This structural absence is key to understanding both human subjectivity and the theological implications of the Cross. The stability provided by the Name-of-the-Father is always something of a fiction—a necessary fiction, but a fiction nonetheless. When the illusion is shattered, the subject is forced to confront the void at the center of meaning. In the case of the Passion, this confrontation reaches its apex in Christ's cry of forsakenness. The Son calls out to the Father and hears nothing in return. The supposed guarantee of coherence is revealed to be empty.

To make this concept more tangible, consider an everyday example: Imagine a child who, up until a certain point, believes his parents are omniscient, all-powerful figures who understand the world completely. The parents function as the Name-of-the-Father; they provide a stable framework for reality. But one day, the child witnesses something that cracks this illusion—perhaps seeing a parent break down in tears, admit uncertainty, or fail to protect them. The realization dawns that their authority was never absolute, that they, too, are fallible. This moment is often profoundly unsettling, as it forces the child to confront the contingency of meaning itself.

A similar phenomenon can be seen in political or ideological structures. A citizen who grows up believing in the absolute righteousness of their country's laws and leaders may experience a moment of profound disillusionment when exposed to systemic corruption or betrayal. The symbolic authority that once seemed unshakable is revealed to be contingent, flawed, or even fraudulent. The result is not just disappointment but a kind of existential vertigo—the feeling that the structures which made sense of the world are no longer reliable.

This is precisely what the Cross dramatizes on a cosmic scale. The Son calls upon the Father, and the expected response—the validation of divine authority—is absent. The Name-of-the-Father does not stabilize meaning; instead, it is revealed to be lacking.

For traditional Christian theology, the Cross is the site of atonement, where Christ's suffering and death reconcile humanity to God. But in a Lacanian reading, the Cross does something even more radical: it forces the subject to confront the abyss of meaning itself. It is not just that Christ dies; it is that he dies without symbolic resolution. The expected narrative of divine intervention is interrupted, leaving only silence.

This moment of symbolic breakdown does not, however, lead to pure nihilism. Rather, it opens the possibility of something beyond the Name-of-the-Father, beyond the previous structures of meaning. Lacan would say that true desire emerges not within the confines of the Symbolic but in its gaps, its failures, its ruptures. In theological terms, this rupture prepares the way for something new—not a return to the old certainties of divine authority but an encounter with something wholly other.

The Cross, in this reading, is not simply an event of suffering, nor even just an act of redemption. It is the crisis of meaning itself, the moment when the Name-of-the-Father is exposed as lacking. Christ does not merely suffer physically; he experiences the ultimate psychoanalytic trauma—the failure of the Symbolic Order that was supposed to sustain him.

But this is not where the story ends, of course. If the Cross is the site of radical destitution, it is also the place where new meaning begins—not a meaning grounded in fixed structures, but one that arises from radical openness to the Real. In the next section, we will see how the Cross does not just leave us in despair but forces a new confrontation with the gaze, the subject, and the nature of divine love itself.

The Gaze and the Cross— Being Seen in Abandonment

We have just seen how the Cross destabilizes the Symbolic Order through the collapse of the Name-of-the-Father. Now, we turn to another foundational Lacanian concept: the gaze. In psychoanalysis, the gaze is not merely about looking; it is about being seen. It is about the unsettling realization that we are objects in the field of the Other, subjected to a vision that comes from beyond us, shaping our identity in ways we cannot control.

Lacan's famous formulation—"I see only from one point, but in my existence, I am looked at from all sides"[10]—captures this unsettling dynamic. To be seen is to be exposed. It is to become an object rather than a subject, to realize that our self-image is mediated by the Other's perception. This is why moments of being watched, whether by another person, a camera, or even an imagined observer, provoke anxiety. The gaze is not something we control—it emanates from the world, from the Symbolic, from the Real.

Nowhere is this experience more profound than on the Cross. Christ is publicly displayed, fully exposed to the gaze of the world. Unlike other executions, which sought to eliminate criminals quietly, crucifixion was designed as a spectacle—an event meant to be seen. The suffering body is turned outward, subjected to mockery, voyeurism, and judgment. The Crucified is not just a victim; he is an object of scorn, reduced to a spectacle of shame.

Pasolini understood this with devastating clarity in *The Gospel According to St. Matthew* (1964). Unlike other Jesus films that either soften the crucifixion or turn it into mere spectacle, Pasolini's camera holds unflinchingly on Christ's face in extreme close-up. We see every bead of sweat, every grimace of pain. The stark black-and-white photography and amateur actors strip away any Hollywood gloss, forcing us to confront the raw reality of being-seen-in-suffering. In one particularly haunting sequence, the camera slowly pans across the faces in the crowd—some mocking, some indifferent, some devastated—while Christ hangs exposed to their collective gaze.

The gaze here is not neutral. It is filled with hostility, contempt, and misunderstanding. The Roman soldiers look upon him with amusement; the religious authorities with satisfaction; the crowd with either indifference or cruelty. Even those closest to him—his disciples, his mother—can do nothing but look upon his suffering. Christ, in this moment, does not merely suffer physically; he suffers the existential trauma of being completely seen in his abandonment.

Perhaps no artwork captures this more powerfully than Matthias Grünewald's *Isenheim Altarpiece* (ca. 1512–1516). Painted for a hospital that treated skin diseases, the altarpiece depicts Christ's body covered in sores similar to those suffered by the patients. His flesh is green with decay, his fingers twisted in agony. But it's the face that arrests us—contorted in pain, mouth agape in a silent cry. Grünewald forces us to see and be seen by this suffering Christ. The patients who gazed upon this altarpiece would have recognized their own afflictions transformed into something both terrible and sacred. Here, the gaze works in both directions—we look upon Christ's suffering, but his suffering also looks back at us.

In Lacanian terms, this is an encounter with the Real of the gaze. It is the moment when all symbolic protections fall away, when the subject is no longer shielded by titles, narratives, or social roles. The one who was called Messiah, Teacher, Son of David is now nothing but a dying body, exposed to the indifferent eyes of the world.

To understand the profound psychological weight of this exposure, consider the experience of shame. Shame occurs when one becomes too visible, when something meant to be hidden is suddenly exposed. Imagine giving a speech and realizing midsentence that you have mispronounced a word in a way that makes the audience laugh at you. Imagine being caught in a deeply personal moment, only to realize that someone has been watching. That burning sensation, that desire to look away or disappear, is the force of the gaze at work.

The Cross magnifies this experience infinitely. Christ cannot look away. He cannot hide. He is completely visible, and yet completely powerless. The gaze of the world is fixed upon him, but the one gaze he seeks—the gaze of the Father—is absent. If shame is the feeling of exposure before the Other, then the Cross is the most radical moment of exposure possible: to be seen by the whole world, while the one who matters most is nowhere to be found.

This brings us to the ultimate paradox. The gaze of the crowd is inescapable, but the gaze of the Father—the divine recognition, the affirmation of identity—is gone. In theological terms, this is the mystery of Christ's abandonment. But in psychoanalytic terms, it is something even more unsettling: the moment when the subject realizes that the Other does not guarantee meaning.

Lacan often spoke of the big Other—the symbolic system that provides coherence, law, and meaning. For a believer, God functions as the ultimate big Other, the final guarantee that meaning is real, that suffering is not absurd, that justice will prevail. But on the Cross, Christ enters into a space where even this guarantee is withdrawn. There is no divine voice affirming his identity. No intervention. No symbolic rescue.

The theologian Hans Urs von Balthasar called this moment "the descent into the second death"[11]—a reference to the idea that Christ experiences not just physical death, but the existential terror of absolute forsakenness. The gaze of the Father is not there to meet him. The world sees him, but he is not seen by the one whose gaze gives life.

The Wound That Sees, the Gaze That Redeems

And yet, paradoxically, it is precisely in this moment of utter exposure that something new emerges. The Cross does not just place Christ under the gaze of the world; it reverses the structure of the gaze itself. The one who is seen in shame becomes the one who sees in love.

The medieval mystics understood this profound reversal. Julian of Norwich, in her *Revelations of Divine Love*, describes Christ's gaze from the Cross as simultaneously wounded and healing. "The eyes of our Lord looked into heaven," she writes, "for his Father's help was full near."[12] Even in abandonment, even when the Father's gaze seems absent, Christ's own gaze remains active, transformative. For Julian, the wounds of Christ become windows—points where divine love peers out into the world, meeting our gaze with infinite tenderness.

Christian mysticism has long meditated on the eyes of the Crucified. Even in death, Christ's gaze remains. In many icons and paintings, Christ's half-closed eyes suggest a seeing beyond—a vision that is no longer fixed within the coordinates of ordinary perception. This is where the logic of the gaze is transformed. The one who is utterly abandoned becomes the one who sees without judgment, without condemnation, without shame.

Lacan reminds us that the gaze is not simply oppressive; it is also revelatory. In the experience of being seen, something about the subject is disclosed—something that remains hidden in the usual flow of life. In the Cross, we see a gaze that sees us in our most abject state and does not turn away. Unlike the gaze of the world, which looks upon the suffering Christ with scorn or indifference, the gaze of the Crucified sees with absolute clarity and absolute love.

The Cross, then, is the site of two opposing gazes. One is the gaze of the world—cold, judgmental, filled with either mockery or indifference. This is the gaze that shames, that isolates, that exposes without mercy. But there is another gaze, the gaze that emerges from the Cross. It is the gaze of one who has suffered ultimate exposure and yet sees without condemnation. It is a gaze that does not shame but heals, does not accuse but redeems.

But how is such a gaze possible? What kind of love can emerge from a place of total abandonment, from the site of absolute destitution? To answer this, we must turn to perhaps the most paradoxical of Lacan's statements about love: "Love is giving what one does not have to someone who does not want it."[13] This enigmatic claim, at first glance, seems like a cruel joke, an absurd formulation that negates the very essence of love. But as with all things Lacanian, its meaning unfolds only when we press deeper. What does it mean to give what one does not have? And how does this illuminate the nature of love, especially as revealed in the Cross?

Love as Lack—Giving What One Does Not Have

In the previous section we explored the gaze—the way the Cross exposes and transforms vision. Now we turn to perhaps the most paradoxical of Lacan's statements about love: "Love is giving what one does not have to someone who does not want it." How do we make sense of this line?[14]

For Lacan, love and desire are always structured around lack. Unlike the romantic ideal that suggests love is about completion—finding one's "other half" or achieving unity—Lacan insists that love is defined by absence. We do not love because we are whole; we love because we are missing something. Love is an attempt to address that missing piece, though never in a way that fully satisfies.

Jean-Luc Nancy, in his meditation on "Shattered Love," pushes this insight even further. Love, he suggests, does not simply lack completion—it actively shatters any attempt at wholeness. "Love," he writes, "is not sublation . . . it is the crossing of shattered existence."[15] This fracturing is not a failure of love but its very essence. Think of Marguerite Duras's *Hiroshima Mon Amour*, where love emerges precisely at the point of impossibility—between a French woman and a Japanese man in the shadow of nuclear devastation.[16] Their love does not heal the wound of history; it inhabits it.

A useful analogy is hunger. When we eat, we satisfy a biological need, but desire is different. Imagine craving a dish from childhood—one prepared by a long-departed loved one. No matter how closely the dish is recreated, it never quite captures the original. The desire is never fully met. Love, in Lacanian terms, functions similarly: it is an offering from the site of one's own incompleteness.

༄

This brings us to the first part of Lacan's formulation. If love is giving what one does not have, it means that true love does not consist in offering something one possesses, but in offering from the site of one's own lack.

Georges Bataille understood this paradox when he wrote that "eroticism is assenting to life even in death."[17] For Bataille, love is not about possession but about loss—a willing descent into the void of one's own incompleteness. We see this enacted with brutal clarity in Claire Denis's film *Trouble Every Day*, where desire literally consumes its object, leaving only absence. The film suggests that to love is to confront an appetite that can never be satisfied, a hunger that devours itself.

In everyday relationships, we often assume that love is about having something to give—attention, gifts, commitment. But Lacan suggests that the most profound love is not about giving from abundance but from emptiness. Consider the moment a grieving friend breaks down in sorrow. We have nothing to give that will erase their pain—no words, no action can undo their loss. And yet, simply being present, offering one's lack of an answer, becomes the deepest act of love. It is not about fixing but about sharing in lack.

Nowhere is this clearer than in the Cross. Christ does not give wealth, power, or even comfort—he gives himself in total emptiness, in absolute destitution. His love is not a love of completion but a love that enters fully into lack. "He emptied himself" (Phil 2:7), taking the form of the most abandoned, the most forsaken. Love, in this context, is not about fulfillment—it is about making oneself radically available in the space of lack.

※

If the first half of Lacan's statement is difficult, the second half is even more unsettling: love is giving what one does not have to someone who does not want it. Why would love be directed toward someone who does not want it?

The answer lies in the nature of desire and recognition. Love, in its deepest sense, disrupts the structures of self-sufficiency. To truly be loved is to be seen in one's lack, in one's vulnerability. And yet, this is precisely what we resist. We long to be loved, but on our own terms—when we are strong, when we are desirable, when we are whole. To be loved in our brokenness, in our helplessness, can feel unbearable. We do not want love that exposes us—we want love that affirms us as already complete.

This is why the love revealed on the Cross is so radical. It is love offered precisely to those who reject it. Christ's love is not directed toward the worthy, the receptive, the grateful—it is given to the world as it mocks, abandons, and crucifies him. This is love that does not depend on the response of the beloved; it is given freely, without condition, without demand. It is love that pours itself out, even when unrecognized.

Most human love operates within an economy of exchange. Even when given freely, love often carries an unspoken expectation: to be loved in return. We say we love unconditionally, but in reality, love often hinges on reciprocity, on affirmation, on being met halfway.

The Cross reveals a love that breaks this economy of exchange. It is a gift that does not seek return. In psychoanalytic terms, this is a love that does not operate within the logic of the demand—it does not say, "I love you, therefore you must love me back." It is, instead, a pure offering, one that expects nothing.

To use a mundane example: Imagine writing a heartfelt letter to someone you love, expressing your deepest feelings. Now imagine never sending it. The love in that letter exists without expectation, without return—it simply is. The Cross is the ultimate unsent love letter: love poured out, fully given, even when it is refused.

If love is about lack, then love is not a remedy—it is a wound. To love is to be opened, to be made vulnerable, to risk loss. This is why love and suffering are so intimately connected. In Lacanian terms, love does not resolve the subject's incompleteness; it exposes it even more fully.

This is profoundly unsettling. It means that love does not offer security in the way we often hope it will. It means that to love is not to be completed but to be undone. It is no coincidence that in mystical theology, encounters with divine love are often described in the language of wounds—St. John of the Cross's "wound of love," or Teresa of Avila's vision of an angel piercing her heart. The Cross embodies this paradox: love that does not remove suffering, but love that enters into suffering fully.

Lacan's formulation—"Love is giving what one does not have to someone who does not want it"—finds its ultimate expression in the Cross. Christ gives, not from a place of abundance, but from the most radical emptiness. He offers love to those who reject it. And in doing so, he reveals a love that is not about possession, not about completion, but about the absolute gift of the self in lack.

This is a love beyond transaction, beyond economy. It is a love that does not seek to fill a void but embraces the void itself. It is the love that sees us in our most broken state and does not turn away.

Living in the Wake of the Cross— Faith Beyond Certainty

If the Cross, as we have explored, is the site of rupture—of meaning's collapse, of love as lack—then what does it mean to live in its wake? If the Name-of-the-Father has been destabilized, if the gaze of the Other no longer offers secure affirmation, if love is a gift given from emptiness, then what remains? How does one inhabit a world after the Cross?

The poet Ingeborg Bachmann, writing after the catastrophes of the twentieth century, captures this dilemma with stark precision. In her poem "Early Noon," she describes a moment of unbearable exposure—standing fully revealed in one's own light, stripped of any protective shadow.[18] This is what it means to live after the Cross—to stand in a light that offers no shelter, no comfortable shade of certainty. Like Samuel Beckett's characters who go on despite knowing they cannot go on, faith after the Cross persists precisely where persistence seems impossible.

In traditional theological accounts, faith is often framed as belief in revealed truths, an acceptance of divine teachings that offer coherence and understanding. But in the wake of the Cross, faith appears as something more unsettling, something less about certainty and more about an openness to the unknown.

Kierkegaard spoke of faith as a leap—not a rational conclusion, not a comfortable resting place, but a movement beyond security. This resonates deeply with the experience of the Cross. The disciples expected a Messiah who would establish an earthly kingdom, a figure of power who would fulfill promises in a way that made sense. Instead, they witnessed total abandonment, a figure who cried out to a Father who did not respond.

The Russian filmmaker Andrei Tarkovsky understood this kind of faith profoundly. In *Stalker* (1979), his characters journey through a mysterious Zone where normal rules of reality don't apply, seeking a room that supposedly grants one's deepest wishes. Yet when they finally reach it, they cannot enter. Their faith is not in the fulfillment of wishes but in the journey itself—a perfect image of what it means to live after the Cross. The Zone, like faith, demands not understanding but surrender to its mysterious logic.

To have faith after the Cross is not to return to the old certainties, to seek comfort in theological systems that pretend the rupture never happened. It is to inhabit the rupture, to dwell within the space of unknowing, and yet to persist. Faith, in this sense, is not a possession but an ongoing act, an endurance in the face of radical uncertainty.

The Spanish poet José Ángel Valente speaks of this in his later work, describing faith as the hand that reaches out into emptiness.[19] Not to grasp something, but to remain open in the gesture of reaching. This is what Cardinal Nicholas of Cusa meant by his *docta ignorantia*—learned ignorance—a wisdom that consists not in knowing but in a deeper understanding of not-knowing.

If faith after the Cross is not about certainty, then what sustains it? The answer, paradoxically, is love—but not love as completion, as fulfillment, as possession. Faith is sustained by love as lack, by love that remains even when meaning fails.

CRUX

Lacan's insight that love is giving what one does not have takes on new depth in this context. To live after the Cross is to love without guarantees, to persist without the certainty of return. It is the faith of Mary Magdalene at the empty tomb, weeping in confusion yet refusing to walk away. It is the faith of Peter, shattered by his own denial, yet still leaping into the sea when he sees Christ on the shore. It is the faith of Thomas, who doubts but does not leave, who demands to touch the wounds—not as proof, but as an encounter with something real.

The contemporary composer Arvo Pärt captures this paradoxical persistence in his *Stabat Mater* (1985). The piece begins with silence, is built around silence, returns to silence. Yet the silence is not empty—it is charged, expectant, like the space left by absence. This is how faith persists after the Cross: not by filling the void, but by learning to inhabit it.

Faith, then, is not about having answers but about remaining open. It is not about resolving the trauma of the Cross but about dwelling within it, allowing it to reshape what love and subjectivity mean. It is about stepping forward, even when there is no clear path, about trusting not in certainty but in the possibility of something beyond it.

To live in the wake of the Cross is to live without resolution, to embrace a faith that does not seek to restore old structures of meaning but instead creates space for something new. It is to recognize that love is not about fulfillment but about gift, that subjectivity is not about wholeness but about openness, that faith is not about certainty but about endurance.

The Cross does not offer easy answers. It does not promise a return to the security of the Symbolic Order. What it offers instead is a transformation of vision, a reconfiguration of love, an undoing that makes something new possible. To follow the Crucified is not to find stability but to step into the unknown, to risk everything for a love that lacks, for a faith that persists, for a life that is not grounded in possession but in gift.

And so, we return to where we began—not with a conclusion, not with a resolution, but with an invitation: to stand before the Cross, to let it undo us, and to step forward anyway.

Chapter Two

Faith Against Itself
Žižek

In 2012, Slavoj Žižek stood before an audience and spent twenty minutes analyzing a can of Coca-Cola. Not its ingredients or corporate history, but the strange paradox of drinking it. When you're thirsty, he observed, Coke is never quite enough—it's too sweet, too fizzy. It doesn't really quench thirst; it creates a new kind of thirst. "The more you drink it, the more thirsty you get," he declared, tugging at his T-shirt with characteristic nervousness. "Your thirst is like the desire of vampires for blood—the more they drink it, the more they want it. The perfect commodity—the more you consume it, the more you need it!"

Behind the audience's laughter lay a profound point about desire, satisfaction, and the void at the heart of our consuming passions. Such moves define Žižek's approach: taking something seemingly trivial—a soft drink, a joke, a scene from a Hollywood movie—and revealing how it illuminates the deepest philosophical and political questions.

Since emerging from relative obscurity in Slovenia to become an unlikely global intellectual celebrity, Žižek has broken every rule of academic discourse. He sniffs, twitches, interrupts himself, tells dirty jokes, and peppers his lectures with references to Hollywood films and Soviet jokes. Yet beneath this eccentric exterior

FAITH AGAINST ITSELF

lies one of contemporary philosophy's most original minds. His work draws together Hegelian philosophy, Lacanian psychoanalysis, and radical political theory to produce insights that are both deeply unsettling and surprisingly relevant to our current moment.

Perhaps nowhere does Žižek's peculiar genius shine more brightly than in his analysis of Christianity. Once again, he begins with what seems like pure provocation: "Only an atheist can be a true Christian."[20] The statement appears designed to irritate everyone—believers and nonbelievers alike. Yet just as with the Coca-Cola analysis, the seeming joke opens into something profound. For Žižek, Christianity contains resources for radical thinking that neither conventional faith nor conventional atheism can match.

What makes Žižek›s approach so powerful is how he weaves together three seemingly incompatible strands of thought: Hegel's dialectics, Marx's political critique, and Lacan's psychoanalysis. Where Hegel saw how truth emerges through contradiction, where Marx exposed how power structures shape our thinking, and where Lacan revealed the unconscious structures of desire, Žižek finds tools for understanding Christianity's most radical implications.

This isn't just academic game playing. By combining these perspectives, Žižek sees something in Christianity that both believers and critics often miss. Religious readers tend to soften Christianity's hard edges, turning the Cross into a comfort rather than a challenge. Secular critics dismiss it as mere superstition or ideological control. But through Žižek's lens, Christianity emerges as something far more unsettling: a tradition that contains its own subversion, that stages the death of God from within faith itself.

Such theoretical claims might sound abstract until we see them played out in contemporary culture. Consider an unexpected example: In 1985, Nick Cave stalked onto stages like a possessed preacher, howling tales of murder and apocalypse to audiences both terrified and thrilled by his gothic intensity. The son of an

English teacher and a librarian who had taught Bible classes, Cave seemed determined to scandalize every sacred thing he'd inherited. His performances with the Birthday Party and early Bad Seeds felt like exorcisms—sweat-drenched, violent, deliberately blasphemous.

Decades later, Cave sits at a piano during one of his "Conversations with . . ." events. The setting is intimate, the lights low. Someone asks about his faith, perhaps expecting tales of continued rebellion. Instead, what emerges is something stranger, more unsettling than his old theatrics of transgression. He speaks of Christianity with a seriousness that seems to startle the room. "The more I study the actual ideas of Christianity," he says, "the more radical and transformative they become. The more impossible they become."[21]

Far from a typical conversion story—a tale of wildness tamed by faith—Cave suggests something more provocative: his earlier rebellion against Christianity wasn't radical enough. Those youthful blasphemies were, in fact, too safe, too conventional, still operating within the logic they claimed to oppose. Real engagement with Christianity, he implies, is more traumatic than any mere rebellion against it.

What Cave has discovered—and what Žižek's work illuminates with particular force—reveals Christianity's harboring of a truth more radical than any external criticism could muster. "What if," Žižek asks in *The Puppet and the Dwarf*, "Christianity is not just another name for universal moral teaching or an obscure path to inner enlightenment? What if its scandalous core is something far more disturbing?"[22] Traditional religion offers cosmic meaning as compensation for earthly suffering. Conventional atheism celebrates liberation from religious illusion. Yet Christianity, Žižek suggests, does something far stranger: it stages the death of God as an event within faith itself.

Search today's spiritual marketplace, and you'll find no such insights. Meditation apps promise inner peace; self-help gurus offer five easy steps to enlightenment. While "spiritual but not religious" seekers browse for comfortable truths and conspiracy theorists construct grand narratives that explain everything, Christianity insists on confronting what cannot be resolved. As theologian William Lynch observed, authentic faith doesn't lift us above contradiction—it pushes us more deeply into it.[23]

Understanding why Christianity might be more radical than both religion and atheism requires following Žižek's analysis into increasingly unsettling territory. Only by diving deeper can we see how the Cross doesn't just represent divine suffering but stages a more profound trauma: God's own participation in the death of God. Uncomfortable territory, certainly. But then, as Žižek reminds us, tugging at his shirt and sniffing compulsively, truth never is.

Beyond "Spiritual but Not Religious"

Many spiritual frameworks resolve their contradictions neatly. New Age philosophy promises harmony through cosmic oneness. Self-help spirituality offers five easy steps to inner peace. Even contemporary atheism often presents itself as simple liberation from superstition. Each promises, in its own way, to make everything make sense.

Yet what makes Christianity dangerous—truly dangerous, not just culturally controversial—lies in its refusal of such neat resolutions. While modern spirituality offers what philosopher James K. A. Smith calls "therapy for the bourgeois soul,"[24] Christianity confronts us with something more unsettling: a God who experiences godforsakenness, a divine presence that manifests through absence, a truth that shows itself through its own undoing.

Nowhere is this contrast more striking than in contemporary culture's obsession with the paranormal. Žižek notes how the "death of God" hasn't led to pure secular rationality but to an explosion of ghost-hunting shows, paranormal investigation teams, and New Age spiritualism. When traditional faith dissolves, we don't get atheism—we get an anxious multiplication of spirits, energies, and supernatural encounters. Reality TV crews prowl abandoned hospitals with EMF meters. Mediums claim to channel the dead.

Each apparent contact with the beyond promises to fill the void left by God's absence.

This spiritual anxiety extends even into traditional religious communities. Sociologist Christian Smith's research reveals how many young Christians have abandoned orthodox faith not for atheism, but for what he calls "moralistic therapeutic deism"—a vague belief in a cosmic force that wants us to be nice and feel good about ourselves.[25] This isn't merely watered-down Christianity; it's a fundamental transformation of faith into therapy, where divine absence is papered over with comfortable platitudes.

Žižek reserves particular scorn for what he calls "Western Buddhism"—not authentic Buddhist tradition, but its contemporary Western appropriation as spiritual commodity. "Western Buddhism," he writes in *On Belief*, "presents itself as the remedy against the stressful tension of capitalist dynamics, allowing us to uncouple and retain inner peace . . . yet it actually functions as its perfect ideological supplement."[26] The promise of inner peace through mindfulness becomes another consumer product, another way to make ourselves more efficient participants in the very system that creates our anxiety.

A visit to any contemporary Starbucks illustrates his point perfectly. Here, customers don't just buy coffee—they purchase "coffee karma," the vague promise that their overpriced latte somehow contributes to global ethical harmony. The entire "spiritual but not religious" marketplace operates on similar logic: selling transcendence without transformation, wisdom without wound, enlightenment without upheaval.

Christianity, properly understood, refuses such comfortable transactions. It won't sell you spiritual peace. It won't resolve contradictions. It won't make everything make sense. Instead, it drives us deeper into the very tensions we seek to escape.

Scripture's most difficult texts reveal this unsettling quality. The author of Ecclesiastes doesn't just question meaning—he systematically dismantles every attempt to construct it. "Vanity of vanities," he declares (Eccl 1:2), but this familiar translation obscures the Hebrew *hebel*'s more radical connotation: vapor, smoke, absolute emptiness. Here we find no comfortable skepticism, but rather a ruthless demonstration of meaning's collapse from within the tradition itself. Ecclesiastes offers no reassuring theological resolution—only the unbearable weight of transience and loss.

This confrontation with absence echoes through artistic expressions of the void. Consider Anish Kapoor's massive installation *Void Field* (1989)—a series of large stone blocks, each with a seemingly bottomless dark hole carved into its center. Viewers report feeling simultaneously attracted to and unsettled by these voids. The holes resist photography, refuse documentation, deny representation. They pull us in, not with answers, but with the weight of absence.

The church fathers also understood this dynamic with a clarity many modern believers have lost. Gregory of Nyssa, writing in the fourth century, insisted that divine darkness illuminates more profoundly than divine light. "The true vision and knowledge of what we seek," he wrote, "consists precisely in not seeing, in an awareness that our goal transcends all knowledge."[27] Such insights don't offer spiritual comfort—they push us toward a more radical confrontation with the unknown.

Modern conspiracy theories provide a telling contrast. Whether in crude forms like QAnon or more sophisticated varieties of gnostic thinking, these systems promise to explain everything, to reveal the hidden truth behind appearances. They offer what religion traditionally provided: a master narrative that makes sense of suffering, that reveals the pattern behind apparent chaos. But Ecclesiastes—and Christianity at its most radical—moves in the opposite direction. It suggests that the most profound truth might be the absence of any final explanation, any ultimate resolution.

I admit that I find myself both challenged and illuminated by this aspect of the tradition. The temptation always exists to soften Christianity's edges, to transform it into something more manageable, more consoling. Yet the Cross resists such domestication. It confronts us with a truth that cannot be reduced to spiritual self-help or cosmic conspiracy. It demands something more radical than either blind faith or easy skepticism.

CRUX

Christianity's Self-Subversion

Slavoj Žižek has always insisted that the most radical critique of Christianity comes not from the outside, but from Christianity itself. Unlike other belief systems that fortify themselves against internal contradiction, Christianity stages its own undoing at the very core of its message. It is not merely susceptible to critique; it embodies critique. To be a Christian, in Žižek's view, is not to defend faith from attack but to enter more deeply into the vertigo of its own disintegration.

The book of Job provides a crucial example—not just for Christianity, but for the entire theological tradition that precedes it. Often read as a parable of patience in suffering, a demonstration of faith that endures despite hardship, Job actually presents something far more unsettling. Job does not respond to suffering with docile acceptance; he demands answers. He refuses to let God's justice remain an abstract theological given. Instead, he calls God to account—and the response he receives is not comfort, nor explanation, but a whirlwind.

The God who speaks from the whirlwind does not justify himself. He does not explain suffering, does not reassure Job with a cosmic plan. Instead, he speaks of leviathans and wild oxen, of lightning and storehouses of snow. He overwhelms Job not with answers but with the sheer force of mystery. In Žižek's reading, this is not just a display of divine majesty—it is the moment when faith turns back on itself, when Job realizes that the categories he has inherited to make sense of God—justice, order, reward—are not only inadequate but are actively dismantled by God's own speech.

Prophetic voices carry forward this subversive streak. Isaiah does not simply predict future events—he announces God's judgment against empty religious observance: "I have had enough of burnt offerings of rams and the fat of fed beasts; I do not delight in the blood of bulls" (Isa 1:11). Jeremiah doesn't just call for repentance—he accuses God himself: "Why is my pain unceasing, my wound incurable, refusing to be healed? Truly, you are to me like a deceitful brook, like waters that fail" (Jer 15:18). These are not comfortable affirmations of divine order. They are moments when faith confronts its own internal crisis.

Even Jesus's parables function as instruments of destabilization. The good Samaritan story doesn't just teach compassion—it suggests that true faith might come from those outside the religious establishment. The prodigal son parable doesn't just tell of forgiveness—it ends with the "good" son outside the feast, unable to accept his father's radical grace. Each story sets up traditional religious expectations only to undermine them from within.

But it is on the Cross where this self-subversion reaches its most radical point. Here, in what should be the moment of divine triumph, we find instead the cry of abandonment. The one called the Son of God does not display divine power; he experiences divine absence. This is why Žižek insists that the Cross is not simply an event within Christianity—it is the moment when Christianity confronts its own impossible core.

Meister Eckhart, the medieval mystic, approached this insight when he prayed, "I pray God to rid me of God."[28] At first glance, this sounds like blasphemy. But Eckhart recognized something profound: that our very concepts of God—even our most cherished theological frameworks—must themselves undergo crucifixion. True faith begins not with certainty but with the courage to let our religious securities be stripped away.

As a Catholic thinker, I find myself wrestling with the implications of this insight. While I cannot follow Žižek to his most radical conclusions about divine absence, his reading of Christianity's self-subverting nature illuminates something crucial about authentic faith. It suggests that the truth of Christianity might lie not in its ability to provide answers, but in its willingness to sustain the deepest questions, even when those questions threaten our theological comfort.

Before we move deeper into Žižek's reading of divine self-emptying, however, we need to understand what's really at stake theologically in his interpretation. Contemporary theology often finds itself caught between two extremes. Liberal theology tends to dissolve Christianity's radical elements into general ethical principles, turning the Cross into a symbol of generic compassion. Conservative theology often reduces it to a transaction, a divine payment for human sin. Both approaches, in their different ways, try to tame what Žižek sees as Christianity's most unsettling implications.

Consider how different Christian traditions have wrestled with divine absence. The Carmelite mystic John of the Cross wrote of "the dark night of the soul," where God seems utterly withdrawn. But he saw this absence as temporary, a spiritual trial leading to deeper union. The Reformed tradition speaks of the "hidden God" (*Deus absconditus*), but generally frames this hiddenness as a test of faith. Žižek pushes us toward something more radical: What if divine absence isn't just a spiritual experience or theological concept, but the very truth of Christianity itself?

This is where many readers, especially those committed to traditional faith, might want to stop following Žižek's argument. I certainly recognize the reasons for this hesitation. Yet his provocation forces us to confront questions that lie at the heart of Christian thought: What if God's presence operates precisely through absence? What if faith means not holding onto certainty but entering fully into doubt?

Hans Urs von Balthasar, one of Catholicism's most profound modern theologians, spoke of Christ's descent into hell as "the real theologically decisive center of the whole."[29] For Balthasar, this wasn't just about Christ's suffering—it was about God experiencing godforsakenness. Yet even Balthasar, radical as this insight was, saw it as part of a larger movement toward resurrection and divine triumph. Žižek asks us to dwell longer in the moment of abandonment itself.

The implications are staggering. Traditional theology has always insisted that God cannot change, cannot suffer, cannot be diminished. The divine nature, by definition, must remain perfect and complete. But the Cross seems to tell a different story. What kind of God is revealed in the cry of abandonment? What does it mean that the Word made flesh experiences the silence of God?

Karl Rahner, another giant of twentieth-century Catholic thought, suggested that God's unchangeability might paradoxically include the capacity for self-emptying—that divine perfection might manifest precisely in the ability to enter fully into human limitation. This opens a path for thinking about how God's transcendence might appear not beyond human experience but within it, in the very place where divinity seems most absent.

Yet Žižek pushes even this insight further. For him, the Cross doesn't just reveal a God who voluntarily assumes limitation. It reveals that limitation, absence, and self-emptying are not temporary divine strategies but the very nature of God. This is where many theologians and philosophers must part ways with Žižek's most radical conclusions. But we cannot simply dismiss them. They force us to question whether our traditional theological frameworks have truly reckoned with the scandal of the Cross.

The Structure of Disavowed Belief

Contemporary Christians often maintain their faith through a peculiar form of distance. A believer might say, "Of course I don't literally believe all those miracle stories . . ." while still attending church, still participating in rituals, still identifying as Christian. This is not simple hypocrisy. It reveals something more complex about how belief functions in our supposedly secular age. As Žižek notes, the most common form of belief today is belief held at arm's length—not "I believe" but "I believe through others who believe."[30]

The pattern appears everywhere once we learn to recognize it. Consider how often people preface their religious statements with "I'm not one of those Christians, but . . ." or "I'm spiritual but not religious . . ." These are not mere disclaimers. They reveal a fundamental shift in how belief operates. The modern believer wants to maintain faith while simultaneously displaying sophistication about that faith. Like the moviegoer who knows the special effects aren't real but is moved by them anyway, the contemporary Christian often adopts a position of "I know very well, but still . . ."

Modern disavowal takes many forms. Some treat Christianity as valuable "cultural heritage" while disclaiming its metaphysical claims. Others embrace its ethical teachings while keeping ironic distance from its supernatural elements. Still others participate in its rituals while maintaining they do so "symbolically" rather than literally. Each approach reveals the same structure: belief maintained through its very disavowal.

Yet what makes this position so unstable is not its seeming contradiction but its ultimate inadequacy before the Cross. Here is something that cannot be held at arm's length, cannot be maintained through sophisticated distance. The Cross confronts us with what Žižek calls "the Real" of Christianity—not just an event to be believed or disbelieved, but a trauma that dismantles the very structure of belief and disbelief.[31]

Consider how differently the Cross functions from other religious claims. One can maintain ironic distance from miracle stories, can treat ethical teachings as cultural wisdom, can view rituals as meaningful symbols. But the Cross presents us with something that refuses such comfortable positioning. It is too brutal to be merely symbolic, too senseless to be reduced to ethics, too devastating to be held at sophisticated distance. God dies—not metaphorically, not symbolically, but actually. And this death occurs not despite faith but because of it, not outside belief but at its very center.

The sophisticated believer's "I know very well, but still . . ." crumbles here. There is no position of safe observation, no way to maintain protective distance. Either God dies—really dies, truly dies—or Christianity means nothing at all. This is why Žižek insists that true Christianity requires neither naïve belief nor cynical distance but something far more radical: full exposure to the trauma at its core. The Cross doesn't ask us to "believe"—it demands we enter into God's own participation in the death of God.

Most contemporary attempts to "save" Christianity from its own radicality reveal themselves as elaborate defenses against its core truth. Liberation theology wants to turn the Cross into a symbol of solidarity with the oppressed. Conservative Christianity reduces it to a divine transaction paying humanity's debt. Progressive Christians treat it as a metaphor for self-giving love. Each approach, in its own way, tries to maintain safe distance from what actually happens on the Cross. But the more we try to domesticate this event—to turn it into ethics or politics or mysticism—the more its true horror reasserts itself. What happens on the Cross is not that an exemplary human dies for a noble cause, not that divine justice is satisfied through sacrifice, not that love proves stronger than death. What happens is that God himself enters into godlessness. Divinity experiences its own absence. The absolute becomes nothing. This is not a meaning we can interpret from a distance; it is an abyss into which we must fall.

Here we begin to grasp why both simple belief and sophisticated disbelief miss Christianity's most radical dimension. The naïve believer wants to skip over God's death to reach resurrection. The cynical observer wants to maintain knowing distance from the whole affair. But true Christianity, as Žižek insists, requires something more traumatic than either position: full acceptance that God's own self-negation is not incidental to faith but its very essence.[32] This is not a truth that can be believed while maintaining ironic distance. It must be entered into, experienced, suffered. The Cross shatters both the simple believer's desire for divine guarantee and the sophisticated skeptic's attempt at protective distance. What remains is neither belief nor unbelief but exposure to an event that continues to rupture every framework we use to make sense of it.

This means that authentic Christianity is not, in the end, about finding the right position in relation to belief—neither simple acceptance nor sophisticated distance will suffice. It is about entering into an event that undoes the very structure of believing. The Cross does not require us to "believe" that God died; it demands we participate in God's own death, in divinity's own self-emptying. This is where all our attempts at maintaining safe distance collapse. We cannot observe this event from outside; we can only be drawn into it. And in being drawn in, we discover something that exceeds both belief and unbelief: that God's own self-negation creates the space for a new kind of existence altogether.

These theological questions find their deepest expression in Christianity's most radical concept: *kenosis*, the self-emptying of God. No longer an abstract theological problem, kenosis becomes the key to understanding how divine transcendence might manifest through its own undoing. Here we enter territory so unsettling that even the most adventurous theologians have often retreated to safer ground.

Kenosis and Divine Self-Emptying

At the heart of Christian theology lies a concept so radical that even believers often struggle to grasp its full implications: kenosis, the self-emptying of God. The term comes from Paul's Letter to the Philippians, where Christ is described as having "emptied himself, taking the form of a servant" (Phil 2:7). For most of Christian history, theologians have treated this passage carefully, seeing it as a description of Christ's humility while carefully preserving divine power and authority. But Žižek pushes us toward a more unsettling reading: What if kenosis isn't just about divine humility? What if it reveals something more radical about the nature of God?

Simone Weil, the brilliant and enigmatic French philosopher who died in 1943, provides perhaps the most rigorous thinking about this divine self-emptying. Despite—or perhaps because of—her position on the margins of institutional Christianity, Weil saw with unusual clarity how kenosis undermines traditional religious thought. She developed the concept of decreation, arguing that God's creative act was not one of power but of withdrawal. "God can only be present in creation under the form of absence,"[33] she wrote. Creation itself begins with divine self-limitation, with God making space for something other than God to exist.

For Weil, this divine self-emptying provides the pattern for all authentic spiritual life. Just as God creates by withdrawing, we approach truth not through accumulation of knowledge or power, but through a radical dispossession. Faith becomes not a source of strength but a form of weakness, not a gaining of certainty but a letting go of our demand for it.

Kenosis is not the negation of God's being but its deepest expression. Divine self-emptying does not destroy transcendence; it reveals a love so complete that it willingly withdraws for the sake of the other. Yet Žižek takes this one step further: What if kenosis doesn't just describe how God loves? What if it exposes the very structure of divinity as emptiness itself?

If God truly empties himself in Christ, Žižek argues, then kenosis is not just a temporary strategy of divine humility—it is a permanent revolution in how we understand divinity itself.[34] The Cross doesn't simply show us a God who temporarily assumes weakness; it reveals that divine power manifests itself precisely through self-emptying.

Consider how this reverses our usual theological logic. Traditional religion seeks God in displays of power, in miraculous interventions, in the restoration of order. But kenotic theology suggests something far stranger: that God appears most fully in acts of dispossession, in moments of withdrawal, in experiences of absence. "God's greatness," as the contemporary theologian Rowan Williams puts it, "is demonstrated not in his having all the power all the time but in his capacity to withdraw, to make space for what is not God."[35]

John Cage's famous composition *4'33"* (1952) offers an unexpected artistic parallel to this kenotic logic. The piece consists of a pianist sitting at a piano for four minutes and thirty-three seconds without playing a single note. What might seem like a mere provocation or artistic joke actually enacts something profound: music that emerges not through the assertion of sound but through its withdrawal. The composer empties the space of intentional music, allowing ambient sounds—the shuffling of the audience, the hum of the ventilation system, the sounds of the street outside—to become the composition itself.

Similarly, architect Peter Zumthor's *Bruder Klaus Field Chapel* (2007) embodies kenosis in concrete form. From the outside, it rises from a German field like a stark monolith. Inside, its walls bear the charred imprint of the logs used to shape the concrete during construction—logs that were burned away, leaving only their trace. The space itself was formed through an act of emptying. Visitors often report feeling both exposed and embraced, as if absence itself had taken physical form.

But kenosis is not merely an aesthetic principle or a mystical gesture of retreat. For Žižek, its implications stretch far beyond art and architecture—into the very structure of power itself. If divine power is revealed through self-emptying rather than dominance, then the Christian political imagination must confront a profound challenge: What does it mean to wield power while renouncing its coercive force?

Here I find myself both compelled and unsettled by Žižek's reading. Christian tradition has always recognized the paradox of Christ's self-emptying, but Žižek pushes this insight toward an abyss where all religious stability threatens to collapse. If kenosis is not just a moment in divine history but the very nature of divinity itself, then does Christianity still have a God in any meaningful sense? If all that remains is an empty structure of self-negation, at what point does Christianity dissolve into a theology of pure loss? And yet—perhaps this very instability is precisely what the Cross demands we confront.

The Death of God from Within

"Christianity is much more atheist than the usual atheism,"[36] Žižek writes in *The Puppet and the Dwarf*. At first glance, this seems like another of his characteristic provocations. But there's something deeper at work here. For Žižek, Christianity doesn't just acknowledge divine absence—it stages God's death as an event within faith itself. This is not the comfortable atheism that simply denies God's existence. It is the more traumatic recognition that Christianity contains its own atheism.

The Danish filmmaker Carl Theodor Dreyer captured something of this paradox in his masterpiece *Ordet* (1955). The film centers on Johannes, a man who believes himself to be Christ. When tragedy strikes his family, the question becomes unavoidable: Does faith demand belief in the miraculous, or must it endure the silence of God? Throughout the film, Dreyer lingers on moments of stillness and unresolved tension. Faith is neither confirmed nor denied—it hovers in an unbearable space of uncertainty.

Dreyer's film leaves faith suspended in unbearable uncertainty, yet Žižek pushes further: What if this uncertainty is not a waiting period before faith is confirmed, but faith's deepest truth? What if Christianity does not resolve this crisis, but enshrines it at its core?

Žižek finds particular significance in the tearing of the temple veil at the moment of Christ's death. Traditionally, this is read as a sign that Christ's sacrifice has opened direct access to God. But Žižek sees something far more unsettling: not an invitation into divine presence, but the exposure of divine absence. The veil did not merely separate humanity from God; it concealed the terrifying possibility that behind it, there was nothing at all. Its tearing doesn't signify communion—it signifies collapse.

For Nietzsche, the death of God is an act of emancipation—the collapse of religious illusion opens the way for human strength. But for Christianity, the death of God is an act of self-negation. Unlike the Nietzschean atheist, who rejoices in the fall of divine authority, the Christian must stand at the Cross and confront the unbearable truth: God himself undergoes the death of God. Liberation does not follow. No new order emerges. There is only the rupture itself.

This is why the medieval mystics remain so relevant. When Meister Eckhart prays to "be rid of God," he is not rejecting divinity—he is recognizing that our very concepts of God must undergo crucifixion. Yet for Eckhart, this negation is not final. The loss of God does not leave only absence; it creates the space for a deeper presence, a divine reality that can only be encountered beyond conceptual grasp.

CRUX

The Revolutionary Demand

If the Cross reveals divine power through self-emptying, if God manifests through absence rather than presence, then what does this mean for how we live? For Žižek, Christianity's radical core demands more than theological speculation—it requires a fundamental reimagining of human community and political action.

"The only way to be an authentic Christian," Žižek argues in *Living in the End Times*, "is to stake everything on the communist gesture of radical equality."[37] This isn't just provocative rhetoric. If Christianity reveals its truth through self-emptying—through the death of cosmic guarantees—then it demands a radically new way of being in the world. We can no longer wait for divine intervention to solve human problems. The task of transformation falls to us.

Dorothy Day understood this with extraordinary clarity. When critics accused her Catholic Worker Movement of being too political, too focused on material conditions rather than spiritual concerns, she responded by going further. The soup kitchens, the newspaper, the direct action against war and inequality—these weren't distractions from Christian spirituality but its necessary expression. If God reveals himself through self-emptying, through becoming human, then serving humanity in its most material needs becomes the highest spiritual act.

Liberation theology, for all its controversies, pushes this insight to its logical conclusion. When Gustavo Gutiérrez insists that we meet Christ in the poor, he's not being metaphorical. If God manifests through self-emptying, then divine presence is found precisely where worldly power and privilege are absent. This isn't just applying Christian principles to political problems—it's recognizing that Christianity's central insight about divine self-emptying demands political engagement.

Yet Žižek critiques even liberation theology for not going far enough. The point isn't simply to align Christianity with leftist politics. Rather, Christianity's radical core disrupts *all* political orders, including revolutionary ones. The logic of kenosis—the total dispossession of power—undermines every system of power, whether capitalist or socialist. True Christianity doesn't just replace one system with another; it calls for the dismantling of power itself.

This revolutionary demand creates profound tensions for institutional Christianity. Churches often function as preservers of social order rather than agents of radical transformation. They offer spiritual comfort without challenging material realities. But the Cross, properly understood, permits no such compromise. It demands not just personal salvation but the complete reordering of human relationships.

This is where Christianity ceases to be an abstract doctrine and becomes a lived reality. Óscar Romero understood this tension all too well. A bishop who initially sought compromise, he found himself pulled deeper into the suffering of his people in El Salvador, drawn toward a faith that demanded more than spiritual reflection—it required radical solidarity. When he spoke against injustice, he did not do so as a political ideologue, but as a priest standing beneath the Cross, recognizing that Christianity demands a response to the suffering world. "A church that does not unite with the poor to denounce injustice is not the true church of Jesus Christ," he declared.[38] For this, he was assassinated while saying Mass, his body collapsing beside the altar—a modern-day martyr whose death embodied the revolutionary demand of the gospel.

A similar fate awaited Fr. Stanley Rother, an Oklahoma-born Catholic priest who served among the indigenous people of Guatemala during the country's brutal civil war. When death squads began assassinating clergy who were suspected of supporting the poor, Rother was urged to return to safety in the US. He refused. "A shepherd cannot run at the first sign of danger,"[39] he wrote to his diocese. He was murdered in his rectory soon after, his blood soaking into the soil of the people he refused to abandon. Like Romero, Rother understood that the Cross demands more than passive faith—it calls for a love willing to stand, and even die, in the face of oppression.

What emerges from these lives is a Christianity far removed from both conservative moralism and liberal humanitarianism. It offers neither the security of unchanging truth nor the comfort of progressive optimism. Instead, it confronts us with an impossible demand: to live in the aftermath of divine self-emptying, to act in a world where God manifests through absence, to build community not through power but through its relinquishment.

This is not a comfortable conclusion. But then, the Cross was never meant to comfort. It stands as a perpetual challenge to both religious and secular certainties, calling us toward a transformation we can neither fully understand nor refuse.

Romero and Rother understood this, yet even their lives are not final answers. The Cross does not resolve history; it interrupts it. When Christ cries out, "My God, my God, why have you forsaken me?" he voices not just personal anguish but a rupture in the very structure of meaning. This cry echoes through history not as a problem to be solved but as a question that keeps opening, keeps demanding response.

In the end, the Cross stands as Christianity's most radical gift to human thought: not an answer, not a system, not a guarantee, but an event that keeps breaking open what we think we know. It demands we live differently in its wake. Whether we can meet this demand—whether we can bear its implications—remains the question that haunts both faith and philosophy.

Chapter Three
The Unbearable Spectacle
Girard

THE TIDE DRAGS THE bodies away. Nailed to crude wooden crosses in the shallows of the ocean, the condemned hang helplessly, their weight sagging forward, their rib cages struggling to expand against the sheer force of exhaustion. The salt water laps against their punctured feet, a grotesque parody of baptism. The waves rise and fall, granting them only moments to gasp for air before the sea chokes them once again. Their deaths are not quick. They are not glorious. They are slow, humiliating, drawn-out degradations of the flesh. They are public. They are meant to be seen.

This is how *Silence* (2016), Martin Scorsese's brutal adaptation of Shūsaku Endō's novel, depicts the crucifixion of Christian martyrs in seventeenth-century Japan. It is not a triumphant vision of martyrdom. It is a lesson in the mechanics of collective violence. The Jesuit missionaries have been framed not merely as heretics but as an infection, an outside corruption that must be purged. Their execution is not random. It is ritualized, theatrical, and necessary—not for the sake of justice, but for the sake of order.

The scene is unbearable to watch precisely because it exposes something we would rather not see: our own need for spectacle, our own participation in ritual violence. Even as we recoil from the horror, something draws us to watch. This same disturbing dynamic played out on a June morning in 1939, at what would become France's last public execution. Hundreds gathered in Versailles to watch Eugen Weidmann die by guillotine. They climbed trees and lampposts for a better view. Some brought cameras, their flashbulbs popping in the predawn darkness. Children were hoisted onto shoulders. The crowd's excitement was palpable—until the blade fell. The spectacle proved too real, too shocking for even a society that considered itself civilized. The photographs, published in the next day's papers, forced France to confront its own appetite for ritualized killing. Public executions were banned shortly after.

René Girard saw this pattern not as an occasional historical atrocity but as the very foundation of human civilization. The mechanism is simple: when tensions rise within a community—whether due to political unrest, plague, famine, or social instability—a scapegoat is selected, marked as guilty, and sacrificed in order to restore harmony. "Violence is not to be denied," Girard writes in *Violence and the Sacred*, "but it can be diverted to another object, something it can sink its teeth into."[40] The victim must be visible. The punishment must be spectacular. And most importantly, the community must believe it is necessary.

The Romans understood this perfectly. Crucifixion was not merely execution—it was theater. They lined their roads with crosses, each victim carefully positioned to maximize visibility. The message was clear: this is what happens to those who disturb the peace. The body must be displayed, must be seen struggling for breath, must serve as a warning. There is no private crucifixion.

Werner Herzog's documentary *Into the Abyss* (2011) reveals how this logic persists even in our supposedly enlightened age. Interviewing death row inmates and those who oversee their executions, Herzog exposes the ritualistic nature of state killing—the careful protocols, the witnessed death, the need for the community to see justice done. Even when hidden behind prison walls, execution remains a public act, a society's visible assertion of its power to purge what it deems unclean.

But what happens when the victim is innocent?

The Unbearable Spectacle

Here lies the singularity of the Cross. In every myth, every religious system, every social purge, the sacrificed one is believed to be deserving of their fate. But the Passion of Christ unmasks the entire process, exposing the lie at the heart of human violence.

The crucifixion of Jesus is, in the eyes of Rome, a political necessity. In the eyes of the religious elite, it is a defense of orthodoxy. In the eyes of the mob, it is justice. "His blood be upon us and on our children!" (Matt 27:25). The crowd believes their violence is righteous, sanctioned, necessary.

In reality, it is murder disguised as righteousness.

The Gospels do not let us look away. They do not frame Christ's death as a mystical ascent or a noble resignation. Instead, they force us to witness what the world does when confronted with the innocent one who refuses to retaliate. Like the drowned martyrs of *Silence*, Christ's crucifixion is designed for public horror. Christ is displayed outside the city gates—a place of exile, a place of refuse, a place where Rome disposes of those it deems unworthy of life.

When Kieślowski filmed *A Short Film About Killing* (1988), he made a devastating choice: depicting the state execution of a murderer in exactly the same brutal visual language as the murder that preceded it. The film forces us to confront how official violence mirrors the very violence it claims to condemn. This is what Girard means when he writes in *Things Hidden Since the Foundation of the World*: "The difference between sacrificial and nonsacrificial violence is anything but obvious. . . . Sacrifice is violence transformed into a technique of healing and, hence, of peace."[41]

But the Cross refuses this transformation. It denies us the comfort of believing our violence is healing anything. Christ's words from the Cross—"Father, forgive them; for they know not what they do" (Luke 23:34)—do not just express divine mercy. They expose the fundamental ignorance at the heart of all sacrificial violence. The persecutors never understand what they are truly doing. They believe they are maintaining order, defending truth, enacting justice. They do not see that they are perpetuating the very violence they claim to remedy.

Girard's insight is devastating: the Cross is not simply an instrument of salvation. It is an indictment. It exposes the foundational lie of human civilization—that peace can be achieved through necessary violence. It reveals that the scapegoat is never truly guilty, only useful.

And if that is true, then what does that say about us?

⁂

Girard's work forces us to wrestle with an unbearable truth: we are still crucifying people today. We have simply refined the method.

The mechanism remains intact—it is embedded in our institutions, our politics, our social media mobs. The stakes are no longer nails and wood, but careers, reputations, and the relentless humiliation of the internet age. We gather, we condemn, we cast out. And we call it justice.

But what if the Cross was meant to end this cycle, not perpetuate it? What if, rather than participating in scapegoating, we are called to stand with the victim?

Girard does not give us an easy way out. He leaves us with a terrifying question: If the Cross reveals the truth of our violence, then how do we live in the wake of that revelation?

To answer this, we must first understand the deeper mechanism at work—not just how sacrifice functions, but why we need it in the first place. We must examine what Girard calls mimetic desire: the force that drives us toward rivalry, violence, and the desperate search for scapegoats. Only by understanding how desire itself becomes violent can we grasp why the Cross poses such a radical challenge to human civilization.

The Deep Logic of Violence

René Girard's genius was in recognizing what had always been hidden in plain sight: we do not desire in isolation. We desire by imitation. Mimetic desire, the force that undergirds all human relationships, drives us to want what others want. We see another's longing, and we internalize it as our own. This is not a passive observation—it is a mechanism as old as humanity itself.

But imitation breeds rivalry. If we want the same things, we will eventually become competitors. Conflict is inevitable. And conflict, if left unchecked, threatens to spiral into chaos. The only way societies have historically contained this violence is through sacrificial violence—by identifying a scapegoat, blaming them for the disorder, and expelling them from the community.

"All our human institutions—law, politics, religion—stem from this ancient act of murder," Girard writes. "They exist to veil the foundational violence on which culture is built."[42] The cycle of collective violence is not an aberration. It is the foundation of civilization itself.

This is why myths, from Oedipus to Romulus and Remus, so often contain a hidden murder—a sacrificial victim whose death purges society of its sins. The myth always insists the victim was guilty, that their punishment was necessary. But the truth is far more disturbing: the scapegoat is always chosen arbitrarily, their innocence irrelevant.

Consider how medieval communities responded to plague. As death spread and social order crumbled, they sought someone to blame. Jews were accused of poisoning wells. Witches were blamed for cursing the land. The pattern was always the same: identify the "source" of corruption, eliminate it through spectacular violence, and restore harmony through bloodshed. What's truly chilling is how effective this mechanism was—not at stopping disease, but at providing social catharsis. After the witch was burned, after the outsider was expelled, a temporary peace would descend. The sacrifice had "worked."

The frightening truth is not just that violence breeds violence—it's that violence is contagious. It spreads from person to person, group to group, nation to nation, each act of retaliation justified by the one that came before it. Blood calls for blood. This is what Girard means when he speaks of "the mimetic nature of violence." We learn whom to hate by watching others hate. We learn whom to blame by watching others blame. The scapegoat mechanism operates through this terrible symmetry—the more people who participate in the accusation, the more "true" it seems.

Social media has made this dynamic horrifyingly visible. Someone transgresses—or is accused of transgressing—and within hours, thousands pile on. The victim's attempts at explanation only fuel the fury. Their past is excavated, their words twisted, their entire existence reduced to a single moment of supposed sin. It doesn't matter if the accusations are true. What matters is that the crowd has found its target. The hunger for sacrifice must be fed.

We know how quickly online mobs can destroy a life. A poorly worded tweet, a video clip taken out of context, an old photo resurfaces—and suddenly someone becomes the embodiment of everything wrong with the world. Their job vanishes. Their reputation shatters. Their family faces harassment. The violence is no longer physical, but it serves the same function: society purges itself through the elimination of a designated victim. The crowd feels righteous. Order is temporarily restored.

But the peace never lasts. This is why Girard insists that sacrificial violence is both necessary and futile. Each sacrifice provides only temporary relief from social tensions. Soon enough, new victims must be found. New scapegoats must be created. The cycle continues, endless and insatiable, because the real source of violence lies not in the victims but in our own mimetic nature—our tendency to desire what others desire, to hate what others hate, to seek salvation through sacrifice.

The Cross interrupts this cycle at its root. It does not merely offer another sacrifice—it exposes the entire mechanism as a lie. When the mob cries, "Crucify him!" they believe they are serving justice, defending tradition, maintaining order. Yet the Gospels strip away these justifications. They show us what we are really doing when we sacrifice the innocent. They force us to see our violence for what it is.

At the heart of Christianity lies a scandal—not just that God becomes human, but that God allows himself to become the scapegoat. The one who is truly innocent submits to the machinery of human violence. But unlike every other sacrificial victim in history, this one speaks. This one names what is happening. "Father, forgive them; for they know not what they do." These words are not just a gesture of mercy—they are a revelation. They expose the fundamental ignorance at the heart of all sacrificial violence.

Consider how differently the Gospels tell this story compared to other ancient accounts of divine death. When Oedipus is cast out of Thebes, the plague ends. When Romulus kills Remus, Rome is founded. The sacrifice "works"—it restores order, brings peace, establishes civilization. But Christ's death refuses such a neat resolution. Instead, the temple veil tears. Rocks split apart. Tombs open. The traditional mechanisms of sacred violence are not confirmed but shattered.

For Girard, the Passion narratives stand utterly unique in human literature. They tell the story from the perspective of the victim, not the persecutors. They refuse to justify the violence. They show us, with unflinching clarity, what we do when our mimetic desires spiral into rage. "In the Passion," Girard writes, "we have the revelation of what has been hidden since the foundation of the world—the truth about collective violence, about sacred violence, about all human culture built on violence."[43]

But if the Cross truly exposes the violent foundation of human society, how can we go on as before? How can we participate in scapegoating once we know what it really is? How can we find peace through sacrifice once we've seen through the lie?

The Cross as the Ultimate Exposure of Our Violence

If Girard is right, then the Cross is not simply the central event of Christianity—it is the greatest rupture in human history. It is the moment when the veil is torn, when the machinery of sacrifice is exposed, when the logic of violence that has governed civilization from its foundations is shattered in real time.

From the outside, the crucifixion appears indistinguishable from any other act of state-sanctioned execution. The Roman world was built on the cross—on public displays of terror, on the bodies of the condemned lining the roads. Yet something happens in this execution that changes everything. The victim does not curse his killers. He does not call for divine wrath. He does not even claim his innocence. Instead, he speaks words that unmake the entire mechanism:

"Father, forgive them; for they know not what they do."

In these words, Jesus reveals the scapegoat mechanism from within. The persecutors do not understand their own actions. They believe they are acting in the name of justice, of law, of religious purity. Yet they are reenacting the ancient cycle of expulsion and murder. Christ's plea exposes their ignorance—it forces them, and us, to confront the terrible truth:

The persecutors always believe they are righteous.

For Girard, this moment is the revelation that no human society can afford to see. If civilization is built upon the sacred lie that violence restores order, then what happens when that lie is exposed? The crucifixion shatters the very foundation of myth. In mythology, the persecuted figure is always guilty—the gods demand their sacrifice, and their death restores balance. Here, in this moment, the victim is innocent, and the gods demand nothing.

Consider how Oedipus's story unfolds: his exile purges Thebes of plague, his suffering becomes noble, his death at Colonus brings blessing. The violence is justified, transformed into sacred necessity. Yet the Passion narrative refuses such transformation. The Gospels do not let us turn Christ's death into a comfortable myth. They force us to watch an innocent man die, abandoned by his friends, mocked by the crowd, crying out to a silent heaven. There is no noble meaning attached to this death, no divine justice served. There is only naked violence masquerading as necessity.

Think about how different mythological narratives handle sacred violence. In the story of Romulus and Remus, the murder of one brother by another becomes the foundation of Rome itself. The violence is not hidden—it is celebrated, transformed into necessity. The death of Remus is not a tragedy but a sacred event that establishes order. The city could not exist without this founding murder. The victim's blood sanctifies the walls.

Or take the Greek *pharmakos* ritual, where cities would maintain a human "scapegoat" to be driven out or killed in times of crisis. The victim would first be fed at public expense, even venerated—then violently expelled or executed. The community's violence was not denied but transformed into sacred duty. The crowd's participation in the murder became a form of purification. This is precisely what Girard means when he speaks of sacrifice's ability to make violence appear necessary, even holy.

The Norse god Odin sacrifices himself to himself, hanging on the world tree Yggdrasil for nine nights to gain wisdom. Even this divine self-sacrifice follows the logic of meaningful exchange—suffering leads to power, death leads to knowledge. The violence is rendered meaningful, part of a cosmic economy of sacrifice and reward.

These myths do not just describe violence—they justify it. They transform murder into meaning. Even when gods die, their deaths serve to establish or maintain order. The violence is never purposeless, never simply brutal. There is always a reason, always a necessity, always a cosmic justification.

The Cross shatters this pattern completely. Christ's death accomplishes nothing in mythological terms. It does not found a city. It does not bring rain. It does not establish cosmic order. Instead, it exposes the emptiness of all such justifications. "My God, my God, why have you forsaken me?" This cry does not transform suffering into meaning—it reveals the horror of trying to create meaning through suffering.

The Gospels, once more, do not let us look away. They do not frame Christ's death as a mystical ascent or a noble resignation. Instead, they force us to witness what the world does when confronted with the innocent one who refuses to retaliate. Isaiah had foreseen this with devastating clarity: "He was despised and rejected by men; a man of sorrows, and acquainted with grief; and as one from whom men hide their faces he was despised, and we esteemed him not" (Isa 53:3). The prophet's words are not just prediction—they are exposure. They reveal how society treats its victims, how we turn away from those we condemn.

Psalm 22 goes even further. "My God, my God, why have you forsaken me?"—the cry that Jesus will echo from the Cross—reveals something that no myth dares to show: divine abandonment itself. This is not the dignified death of a tragic hero. This is not a sacrifice that makes cosmic sense. This is dereliction. Total exposure. The victim's voice rings out, refusing to be silenced: "I am poured out like water, and all my bones are out of joint. . . . They stare and gloat over me; they divide my garments among them, and for my clothing they cast lots" (Ps 22:14, 17–18).

Hans Urs von Balthasar saw in this moment something that most theology tries to avoid. Christ's descent into hell is not just another episode in the salvation narrative—it is, as he writes, "the real theologically decisive center of the whole."[44] The Son experiences not just physical death but the death of meaning itself. He enters into absolute abandonment, into the very darkness that sacrifice was meant to ward off. This is why Balthasar insists that we cannot soften this moment, cannot turn it into a mere transition to glory. The descent must be real. The abandonment must be total.

Balthasar's insight goes even deeper than most readers realize. When he calls Christ's descent into hell "the real theologically decisive center," he's not just making a point about the order of salvation. He's suggesting something that aligns powerfully with Girard's analysis: that divine love must enter into the very depths of human violence—not to sanctify it, but to expose it completely.

In his *Theo-Drama*, Balthasar writes of Christ's experience of God-abandonment as "super-death"—something beyond mere physical death. This is not just suffering, but the experience of absolute rejection, complete abandonment, total exposure to the darkness that sacrifice was meant to keep at bay. Christ enters into what Balthasar calls "the second death"—not just the death of the body, but the death of meaning itself.[45]

This theological insight illuminates why the Cross is not just another sacrifice. In traditional sacrifice, the victim's death is meant to restore meaning, to reestablish connection with the divine. But Christ's death does the opposite—it reveals the absolute emptiness of sacrificial logic. As Girard helps us see, the Cross doesn't create sacred meaning out of death; it exposes how human violence has always hidden behind claims of sacred necessity.

Balthasar suggests that Christ's descent continues until no darkness remains unexposed, until every human attempt to justify violence through appeal to divine necessity is revealed as a lie. This is why he insists that Holy Saturday—the day of God's silence, the day when Christ lies in the realm of the dead—is crucial to understanding the Cross. It is the moment when divine love enters into complete solidarity with victims, when God experiences what Girard calls "the founding murder" from the inside.

This is what sets the Cross apart from every other sacred death in human history. Myths protect us from the truth about violence. They transform murder into necessity, brutality into cosmic order. But the Cross exposes what myths conceal. It shows us not just the physical reality of violence, but its spiritual emptiness. The mechanisms that were supposed to bring peace, supposed to restore order, supposed to connect heaven and earth—they are revealed as nothing but human violence disguised as divine necessity.

And we are left with a haunting question: If the Cross tells us the truth about our violence, then what does that truth demand of us?

Standing with the Victim

The revelation of the Cross leaves us with a choice: once we see the truth about sacrificial violence, we can either turn away or stand with the victims. There is no middle ground. If the Cross exposes the lie at the heart of human violence, then we cannot go on participating in scapegoating as if we don't know what we're doing.

This is what Edith Stein understood in that final moment, on the way to Auschwitz. When she spoke to her sister Rosa—"Come, we are going for our people"—she was not merely accepting martyrdom. She was making a profound choice about which side of the sacrificial mechanism to stand on. As a Jewish convert to Catholicism, she could have emphasized her Christian identity, could have tried to separate herself from those being condemned. Instead, she did the opposite. She identified completely with the scapegoated people, becoming one with those marked for sacrifice.[46]

Stein's action illuminates what Girard means when he writes in *Things Hidden Since the Foundation of the World*: "The Gospels tell us that to escape from sacrifice, we must surrender to the text that has emerged from the sacrificial order, not as one more sacrifice, but as the only discursive space that is foreign to sacrifice."[47] In other words, we must choose to stand with the victim, even—or especially—when doing so makes us victims ourselves.

Franz Jägerstätter embodied this same understanding in a different context. A simple Austrian farmer, he saw with devastating clarity what his nation was becoming under Nazi rule. When called to serve in Hitler's army, he refused. His neighbors thought him mad. Even his priest advised him to think of his family, to go along for their sake. The pressure to participate in collective violence, to join the sacrificial mob, was immense. But Jägerstätter understood something that Girard would later theorize: that Christian faith demands we break with the crowd's unanimity, even at the cost of our lives.

His fellow villagers in St. Radegund could not understand Jägerstätter's stance. "What good will it do?" they asked. "One man cannot stop this war." But their pragmatic objections missed the point entirely. As Girard helps us see, it was never about practical effectiveness. It was about refusing to participate in the machinery of sacred violence, even when that violence wore the mask of patriotic duty. When Jägerstätter wrote from prison, "I can only act according to my conscience . . . I cannot and may not take an oath in favor of a government that is fighting an unjust war,"[48] he was doing more than making a moral choice. He was breaking the unanimous chorus that sacrifice requires.

The cost was everything: Jägerstätter was beheaded on August 9, 1943. But his death accomplished something profound—not by succeeding in worldly terms, but by exposing the lie of sanctified violence. Like Christ's death, his execution revealed what happens when one person refuses to participate in collective murder, when someone steps out of the chorus calling for blood.

In Nagasaki, on that same date two years later, Takashi Nagai would confront an even more staggering test of this truth. A Catholic convert and physician, he survived the atomic bombing only to face an impossible question: How does one respond to the ultimate act of sacrificial violence? The temptation to seek retribution, to demand victims in return, must have been overwhelming. Instead, Nagai did something extraordinary. In his book *The Bells of Nagasaki*, he wrote not of revenge but of divine love, seeing in his city's destruction not a call for retaliation but an invitation to break the cycle of violence completely.

"The atomic bomb," he wrote, "was a great evil. But out of it came the opportunity for us to demonstrate love without seeking revenge."[49] This is not the pious resignation of someone too weak to fight back. It is the radical position that Girard identifies as uniquely Christian—the refusal to answer violence with violence, the decision to stand with victims rather than create new ones.

Nagai went further. He saw Nagasaki's Urakami Cathedral, ground zero for the bombing, as a kind of altar where his fellow Christians had become, in his words, "holy victims . . . chosen as sacrificial lambs, to be slaughtered as unblemished offerings on the altar of sacrifice."[50] But unlike traditional religious interpretations that would sanctify this violence, Nagai's understanding aligns with Girard's insight—these deaths expose rather than sacralize violence. They show us what we do to each other in the name of peace.

CRUX

Nagai's response to apocalyptic violence went beyond personal forgiveness—it offered an entirely new way of seeing catastrophe. As a scientist and a Christian, he refused both the nationalist narrative that would demand vengeance and the victor's narrative that would justify mass killing. Instead, in his tiny hut built from the ruins, he wrote words that would transform how an entire culture understood its wounds.

Nyokodo—his six-foot-square dwelling—became a powerful symbol of his message. The name *Nyokodo*, meaning "As Yourself Hall," came from Christ's command in Luke's Gospel: "Love your neighbor as yourself" (Luke 10:27). But Nagai gave it a specific interpretation. He wrote: "Like it or not, we are all in this together. If you hate others, you're hating yourself. If you kill others, you're killing yourself."[51] This is precisely what Girard means when he speaks of mimetic violence—how aggression against others ultimately destroys the aggressor, how violence consumes everyone it touches.

In his most controversial work, *The Bells of Nagasaki*, Nagai dared to see the bombing as a kind of dark revelation—not because it was good, but because it exposed the ultimate logic of sacrificial violence. The destroyed cathedral, the incinerated Christians, the shadows burned into walls—these were not meaningful sacrifices, but the final exposure of sacrifice's meaninglessness. Yet from this revelation, Nagai drew not despair but an impossible hope: that by seeing violence fully exposed, we might finally choose another way.

This vision cost him dearly. Many Japanese nationalists saw him as a traitor for refusing to call for revenge. Some American observers dismissed him as a naïve pacifist. But Nagai's position was more radical than either side understood. Like Girard's interpretation of the Cross, Nagai's response to Nagasaki was not about passivity in the face of violence, but about breaking its deepest mechanisms. When he wrote about finding burned rosaries in the ruins, their beads fused together by atomic heat, he transformed them into a symbol not of justified suffering but of violence's exposure—and the possibility of living beyond it.

Nagai spent his remaining years—riddled with leukemia from the radiation—living in *Nyokodo*. From this humble dwelling, he wrote books that transformed Japan's understanding of the bombing, not by demanding justice, but by insisting on a love that transcends the logic of sacrifice. This is precisely what Girard means when he speaks of the "intelligence of the victim"—not the wisdom of passive suffering, but the profound insight that comes from refusing to perpetuate violence.

I want to close this section by sharing a powerful set of lines from Seamus Heaney's *The Cure at Troy*, which captures this possibility of breaking free from cycles of vengeance. In one of the most-quoted passages, Heaney's Chorus speaks of rare moments when transformative justice becomes possible, when hope and history align in unexpected harmony. These lines are often invoked in political contexts, but their deeper resonance lies in how they imagine justice without violence, healing without sacrifice. This is not the false peace that comes from finding a scapegoat. It is the harder peace that comes from confronting our own participation in violence.

Heaney's vision extends beyond mere political reconciliation to something more fundamental—what the Chorus describes as a transformative movement beyond vengeance itself, reaching toward genuine healing. This vision of transcending revenge to arrive at authentic transformation, of believing in healing that doesn't require further violence, speaks directly to what the Cross demands of us. It is what Edith Stein enacted in her final solidarity with the condemned, what Jägerstätter demonstrated in his solitary refusal, what Nagai lived out in his transfigured understanding of suffering. Each understood, in their own way, that the Cross does not just reveal the truth about violence—it calls us to live differently in light of that revelation.

The Cross That Haunts

If the Cross exposes the truth about human violence, if it reveals what we are really doing when we create victims, then we cannot pretend we don't know. We can no longer participate in scapegoating with clean hands. The Cross becomes, in Girard's reinterpretation of the biblical phrase, "the stone that the builders rejected" (Ps 118:22; Matt 21:42)—not just a historical event, but a permanent crisis in human consciousness. This is why true Christianity, as Girard insists, is not a religion of order but of disruption. It does not resolve the crisis of humanity—it exposes it. It does not affirm civilization—it reveals its foundational violence. Every attempt to turn Christianity into a force for social stability, every effort to use it to justify new sacrifices, betrays its radical core. The Cross does not stabilize—it destabilizes. It does not comfort—it haunts.

Girard's final works carry an apocalyptic warning: humanity faces a unique crisis. The old sacrificial mechanisms are losing their power to contain violence, but we have not yet learned to live without them. The Cross's exposure of sacrificial violence cannot be unknown, yet we keep trying to make sacrifice work. This is what makes our moment so dangerous—and so full of possibility.

Perhaps this is why the Cross keeps breaking through our attempts to domesticate it. It remains a scandal precisely because it tells the truth about who we are and what we do. It shows us both the depth of our violence and the possibility of another way. It haunts us because it must—because only by being haunted can we begin to imagine a world beyond sacrifice.

In the end, the Cross confronts each of us with a decision. We can turn away from its revelation and continue participating in the old mechanisms of sacrifice, knowing what we know. Or we can accept its haunting—allow it to transform how we see violence, justice, and our own participation in the sacred game of creating victims.

There is no third option. The Cross allows no neutrality. It has exposed what we do to each other in the name of peace, and it keeps exposing us, keeps demanding response, keeps offering the possibility of living differently in the light of its unbearable truth.

Chapter Four

Breaking the Void
Badiou

IN LATE SPRING OF 1968, everything changed. The shift wasn't gradual—it arrived all at once, like a wave crashing against the shore. The streets of Paris convulsed with an energy that defied the ordinary laws of history. A young philosopher named Alain Badiou watched as students occupied the Sorbonne, as workers abandoned their factories, as the foundations of France's social order trembled beneath the force of an Event no one had anticipated. Barricades rose, tear gas choked the air, revolutionary slogans filled the night. But most remarkable was what had never happened before: the fusion of students and workers, intellectuals and laborers—groups whose separation had long seemed natural, inevitable, even structurally necessary. For a fleeting moment, reality itself stammered, revealing possibilities that had always been there but never actualized.

We saw something similar, though less sustained, during the Arab Spring of 2011—particularly in Tunisia's Jasmine Revolution. Like May 1968, it represented a moment when the seemingly impossible suddenly materialized: long-standing dictatorships crumbled, ordinary citizens became revolutionary subjects, and social divisions that had seemed permanent suddenly dissolved.

CRUX

And like 1968, it raised the same questions about Event and aftermath, rupture, and sustainability that would preoccupy Badiou.

And then—it collapsed. History tells us that May 1968 failed. The government regained control, the old order reasserted itself, the revolutionaries were scattered. But for those who had seen what had happened in those weeks, something irreversible had already taken place. What appeared there, Badiou would later suggest, was something that had not been programmed, something that all the rules of the situation forbade. The Event had ruptured the given coordinates of possibility. Even though order returned, reality could never fully close itself again.

Badiou was not merely a participant in the revolutionary fervor of 1968—he was permanently marked by it. The experience of witnessing something truly new in history, something that broke from all existing structures, became the central obsession of his philosophy. But there was a wound here as well. The failure of 1968—its inability to produce lasting transformation—revealed that an Event alone was not enough. The rupture had occurred, but *fidelity* to the Event, the force that would sustain its truth, had faltered. This tension—between the explosive emergence of new possibilities and the fragility of their aftermath—would define Badiou's entire intellectual project.

Many of his contemporaries turned away from radical politics after 1968. Some abandoned the dream of revolution altogether; others dissolved into postmodern skepticism, rejecting the very notion of universal truth. Badiou refused both paths. He insisted that the truth of an Event was not contingent on its immediate success or failure but on the fidelity of those who recognized it. Even if May 1968 had been crushed, it had revealed something undeniable: history is not closed. The possible always exceeds what the present allows. The question was not whether the rupture had been absorbed back into the system, but whether there would be those willing to remain faithful to its implications.

Badiou is, at heart, a philosopher of rupture—of sudden, decisive breaks that reconfigure the very structure of the possible. The world, he argued, is governed by what he called the "state of the situation," the dominant set of rules, assumptions, and exclusions that determines what counts as real, as possible, as meaningful.[52] But every situation contains a void, an element that is present but uncounted, something that does not fit within the system's logic. The Event is what brings this void to light, what forces into recognition that which had been excluded. An Event is not just a political uprising or a moment of resistance—it is the appearance of the impossible within a given order, the eruption of a truth that cannot be assimilated.

This framework helps explain why certain movements fail while others succeed in creating lasting change. Consider the Occupy Wall Street movement of 2011. While it created a genuine rupture in public discourse about economic inequality—introducing terms like "the 1 percent" into common usage—it ultimately struggled to maintain fidelity to its initial breakthrough. Without a sustained commitment to the truth it had revealed, the movement's initial rupture was gradually reabsorbed into the existing system. This is precisely the problem that haunted Badiou after 1968: how to prevent a genuine Event from becoming merely another moment in the system it sought to challenge.

For Badiou, the stakes of this were not merely political or historical but ontological. Truth is not a process of gradual refinement or dialectical synthesis. It does not emerge through debate, compromise, or consensus. Truth arrives as a rupture—an intrusion that cannot be accounted for within the existing framework of knowledge. He was thus in stark opposition to both postmodernism, which sought to dissolve truth into an endless play of perspectives, and traditional metaphysics, which saw truth as something eternal, waiting to be discovered. For Badiou, truth is neither a stable foundation nor a social construct—it is an evental rupture, something that shatters the given coordinates of meaning and demands fidelity from those who recognize it.

This is why Badiou remained a Maoist long after many had abandoned revolutionary politics. Not because he was naïve about Mao's failures, but because he saw in Maoism the radical attempt to remain faithful to rupture. Mao understood that revolution is not a moment but a process, that the real task was not simply to overthrow the old regime but to sustain the new. For Badiou, fidelity was everything. An Event without fidelity is a momentary flash, soon forgotten. Fidelity without an Event is empty nostalgia. The philosopher's task was to understand not only how rupture occurs, but how it can be sustained.

Critics like Slavoj Žižek have argued that Badiou's fidelity to Maoism reveals the central paradox of his thought: How can one distinguish between genuine and false Events? The Cultural Revolution's violence and chaos could be seen as precisely the kind of "illusory rupture" Badiou warns against.[53] Yet Badiou's response is telling: the truth of an Event is not measured by its immediate consequences but by what it reveals as possible. The violence of the Cultural Revolution, he would argue, does not negate the truth it exposed: that radical transformation of social consciousness is possible.

Yet even as he sought to refine his theory of Events, a deeper problem haunted Badiou's thought. If an Event exposes the limitations of a given order, how does one distinguish between a genuine Event and an illusory rupture? If every truth begins as an excess, a disruption, what prevents truth from dissolving into chaos? And most crucially, if fidelity is what sustains the Event, what sustains fidelity itself?

Mathematics and the Real

In 1874, a German mathematician changed the world—not through revolution or war, but through a discovery so radical that it shook the very foundations of reason. Georg Cantor proved that some infinities are larger than others. This was not just a technical insight. It was an ontological rupture, an Event in the history of thought that forced reality itself to be reconsidered. The infinite, which had long been treated as an abstract ideal or an unknowable limit, suddenly fractured into multiple, measurable orders. The very fabric of being had to be reimagined.

Breaking the Void

The brilliance of Cantor's proof lay in its elegant simplicity. He showed that even if you tried to pair every natural number (1, 2, 3 . . .) with a real number (like π, $\sqrt{2}$, or 0.333 . . .), you would always miss infinitely many real numbers. It was like discovering that infinity itself could be measured and compared. This wasn't just clever mathematics—it was a philosophical earthquake. If even infinity could be exceeded, what other supposedly absolute limits might be illusory?

Cantor's discovery was met with hostility. Many of his contemporaries rejected it outright. The influential mathematician Leopold Kronecker denounced him as a "scientific charlatan" and a "corrupter of youth." Others accused him of practicing a kind of mathematical heresy, an affront to the purity of rational thought. Cantor himself suffered deeply, battling periodic breakdowns that left him confined to sanatoriums for much of his later life. But the implications of his work were undeniable: reality contains more than any system can count or fully represent. The excess is irreducible.

We see similar reactions today when fundamental assumptions are challenged. Consider the resistance to quantum mechanics, where particles can exist in multiple states simultaneously, or the ongoing debate about artificial consciousness. Like Cantor's critics, many instinctively reject ideas that threaten our basic understanding of reality. The parallel is striking: just as Kronecker couldn't accept different sizes of infinity, many today cannot accept that consciousness might emerge from computation, or that physical reality might be fundamentally indeterminate.

This is precisely what fascinated Badiou. For him, mathematics is not just a tool for describing reality; it is ontology itself—the only discipline capable of speaking about "being *qua* being" without ideological distortion. Where traditional metaphysics had sought a stable ground for reality, Badiou argued that Cantor had revealed the opposite: being is fundamentally unstable, composed of irreducible excesses and voids that cannot be fully grasped by any conceptual system.

CRUX

This position puts Badiou in fascinating dialogue with the medieval tradition, particularly Aquinas's assertion that God is pure being itself (*ipsum esse subsistens*). But where Aquinas saw mathematical truth as a reflection of divine reason, Badiou inverts this: mathematics itself is the only access we have to being's structure. Yet both recognize that mathematical truth reveals something beyond mere calculation—it touches the real itself.

Cantor's infinities demonstrated something Badiou would seize upon: truth does not emerge through accumulation or synthesis but through rupture. When Cantor proved that the set of real numbers was larger than the set of natural numbers—that some infinities exceeded others—he did not do so by building upon past knowledge in a gradualist fashion. He forced mathematics to confront something that had previously been impossible to think. The old categories could no longer contain the new reality. A break had occurred, and there was no turning back.

This is the structure of an Event. Whether in politics, art, love, or science, truth is not a slow unfolding of what was already there. It erupts. It forces itself upon thought, shattering the existing framework. In this, mathematics and revolution share the same logic: they reveal that what we assumed was necessary was, in fact, contingent. The limits we take for granted can be broken. The impossible is not just possible—it is necessary.

Badiou insists that every situation—whether political, scientific, or personal—contains what he calls a void: something that remains uncounted, unaccounted for, unseen within the existing system. This void is not simply an absence; it is the site of potential rupture. When an Event occurs, it does not emerge from the dominant order. It erupts from the void itself, forcing recognition of something that had always been there but had remained unspoken, unrecognized.

Cantor's infinities are a perfect model for this. Before his discovery, mathematical reality was seen as a single, unified totality. But Cantor revealed that reality is always in excess of what we can represent. There is always more. This "more" is not a supplement or an addition—it is a fundamental condition of being itself. The void is not empty; it is pregnant with uncountable possibilities.

This has radical consequences. If reality always contains more than the present order can account for, then every system is inherently incomplete. There is no final, finished structure of truth. There is always something that remains unassimilated, something waiting to disrupt the whole. In politics, this means that no system can ever fully totalize reality; there will always be an excluded part, a remainder that resists. In art, it means that true innovation comes not from refinement but from rupture—from the creation of something that defies previous forms. In love, it means that genuine fidelity is not about maintaining a stable relationship but about remaining open to the Event of the other, to the possibility of transformation.

Critics like John Milbank have argued that Badiou's mathematical ontology ultimately fails to account for qualitative difference—that by reducing being to set theory, he loses the richness of actual existence.[54] But this misses Badiou's point: mathematics doesn't reduce reality; it reveals reality's inherent excess. The uncountable infinity of real numbers doesn't simplify existence—it shows how reality always exceeds our attempts to grasp it.

Truth Procedures and the Forms of Event

This mathematical insight—that reality always harbors an uncountable excess—provides Badiou with a model for understanding how truth operates across all domains. Just as Cantor's discovery revealed different orders of infinity, Badiou identifies four distinct fields where Events can occur: politics, art, science, and love. Each domain has its own way of encountering the void, its own manner of registering excess, its own procedure for maintaining fidelity to truth.

It's easy to see how differently rupture manifests in each sphere. In politics, the void appears in the uncounted masses, those whose existence the system acknowledges but whose voice it cannot recognize. May 1968 was an Event precisely because it forced these invisible elements into visibility—students and workers whose coalition was "impossible" suddenly appeared as political subjects. In art, the void emerges in forms that cannot be represented within existing aesthetic frameworks. *The Rite of Spring* (1913) didn't just push musical boundaries; it revealed that music itself exceeded what was thought possible. Science encounters its void in phenomena that cannot be integrated into current theoretical paradigms—quantum mechanics didn't merely add to physics; it showed that reality itself was stranger than our categories could contain. And love? Love's void appears in the very impossibility of the encounter—how two separate trajectories suddenly cross, creating something that neither subject could have produced alone.

What makes mathematical thinking so crucial here is that it helps us understand why some Events create lasting transformation while others fade. Just as Cantor's proof of different infinities didn't simply add new numbers but fundamentally altered what we understood numbers to be, a genuine Event doesn't merely add new content to a situation—it transforms the very structure of what is possible. This is why May 1968 remains significant even though it "failed" politically. Like Cantor's discovery, it revealed something that couldn't be unrevealed, even if its immediate implications weren't fully realized.

The mathematical model also illuminates why fidelity to an Event is so crucial—and so difficult. When Cantor proved that some infinities were larger than others, this truth didn't automatically sustain itself. It required mathematicians willing to pursue its implications, to develop new theoretical frameworks, to remain faithful to this rupture in mathematical thought even when the mainstream rejected it. Similarly, political truth requires militants, artistic truth requires creators, scientific truth requires researchers, and love's truth requires lovers—subjects who don't just witness the Event but commit themselves to working out its consequences.

Yet here we begin to grasp something even more radical about Badiou's conception of truth. Just as mathematical truth isn't simply a matter of correct calculation but of encountering what exceeds calculation itself, truth in any domain isn't about accurate representation of what exists. It's about maintaining fidelity to what appears impossible within the current coordinates of existence. This is why he insists that every truth is essentially a multiplicity—not because truth is relative, but because like Cantor's different orders of infinity, truth always exceeds our attempts to grasp it as a unified whole.

This understanding transforms how we view the relationship between different types of Events. Political revolution, artistic creation, scientific discovery, and amorous encounter are not simply analogous—they are different procedures for encountering the same fundamental truth: that reality always contains more than any given situation can represent. Each domain has its own way of registering this excess, its own method for maintaining fidelity to what it reveals. But all share this basic structure of rupture and aftermath, of impossible emergence and sustained commitment.

Mathematical thinking also helps us understand why Events cannot be manufactured or predicted. Just as Cantor's discovery wasn't a logical development of existing mathematics but a rupture that reconfigured mathematical thought itself, genuine Events don't emerge through gradual evolution or planned intervention. They erupt from the void that every situation contains but cannot acknowledge. This is why revolutionary parties so often fail to create real political Events, why artistic movements cannot simply decide to transform aesthetics, why scientific paradigm shifts cannot be scheduled, why love cannot be engineered. The Event's temporality is always that of the already happened—we recognize it only in its aftermath, when the impossible has already become actual.

Moreover, mathematics reveals something crucial about how Events relate to knowledge. Cantor's discovery didn't just add new information to mathematics; it showed that what we thought we knew about infinity was fundamentally incomplete. Similarly, a genuine Event doesn't merely provide new knowledge within an existing framework—it transforms the very conditions of knowing. This is why May 1968 wasn't just a political uprising but a reconfiguration of what "politics" could mean, why *The Rite of Spring* didn't just change music but altered what could be recognized as music, why quantum mechanics didn't just add to physics but revolutionized what we understand as physical reality.

This mathematical model of truth—as something that exceeds while transforming our categories of understanding—will prove essential for grasping what happens in the most radical Event of all: the Resurrection. But before we can approach that impossible irruption, we must first understand more precisely how Events unfold in time, how they generate their subjects, and how fidelity sustains their truth.

The Anatomy of an Event

Badiou insists that truth does not emerge from within the given order; it erupts from without. A genuine Event is not a modification or progression within an existing framework—it shatters the framework itself. It forces recognition of something that had been structurally excluded, something that the previous system could not even account for.

Consider *The Rite of Spring*. When Stravinsky's ballet premiered in 1913, it was not merely a new musical composition. It was an Event. The audience rioted—not because of a single dissonance or an unexpected rhythm, but because the entire foundation of what was recognizable as "music" had been ruptured. The language of composition, form, and expectation had been violently rewritten. *The Rite of Spring* was not a variation on the past; it was a break with it. And yet, after the riot, after the rejection, music itself had been transformed. A new fidelity had been demanded, and those who upheld it did not simply preserve the rupture—they participated in the creation of something new.

We might see a similar rupture in the emergence of artificial intelligence—particularly in the moment when ChatGPT was released in late 2022. Like Stravinsky's work, it wasn't just a technological advancement but an Event that forced us to reconceive what we thought possible. The public response—a mixture of wonder, terror, and rejection—echoes the riot at *The Rite of Spring*'s premiere. Both moments revealed that something fundamental had shifted, demanding a new way of thinking about human creativity and intelligence itself.

This is what Badiou means by an Event. It is not simply something that happens. It is something that forces a response, something that creates subjects who remain faithful to it. The world after an Event is not the same as before, and those who recognize it are changed by it. An Event, in this sense, is always a summons, a call to fidelity.

This is why Badiou sees Paul as the paradigmatic subject of truth. On the road to Damascus, Paul does not choose to rethink his worldview; he is seized by something he cannot ignore. He does not rationally decide to follow Christ—he is knocked to the ground, blinded, unmade. He is not the same afterward. The truth of the Event does not come to him as an idea to be entertained but as a force that demands fidelity. His identity is destroyed, and in its place, something new emerges. "I have been crucified with Christ; it is no longer I who live" (Gal 2:20). Paul does not simply adopt a new ideology; he is made into someone new.

This transformation echoes throughout Christian history. Consider Thomas Merton's experience at the corner of Fourth and Walnut in Louisville, when he was suddenly struck by an overwhelming love for all the people around him. Like Paul, he didn't choose this moment—it seized him. "There is no way of telling people," he wrote, "that they are all walking around shining like the sun."[55] The Event had transformed not just his perception but his very mode of being.

For Badiou, this is the key to every true Event. The subject does not preexist the truth—it is created by it. Truth is not simply a discovery within the existing coordinates of knowledge; it is an interruption that forces the emergence of a new fidelity.

But here, Badiou's framework begins to tremble. He recognizes the radicality of Paul's transformation, yet he insists that truth must remain materialist, that it must belong to the realm of history and politics rather than metaphysics or transcendence. This

CRUX

is where his critique of Christianity begins—he sees Paul's fidelity to the Resurrection as the first great militant truth procedure, but he cannot accept that the Event Paul encountered was real in any ontological sense. For Badiou, the Resurrection must remain a subjective break, not an objective transformation of reality itself.

And yet, Paul does not speak of choosing fidelity to the Event. He speaks of being grasped. "Not that I have already obtained this or am already perfect," he writes, "but I press on to make it my own, because Christ Jesus has made me his own" (Phil 3:12). This is not the language of a subject constructing truth—it is the language of one who has been claimed by it.

Badiou understands how an Event generates subjects, but he cannot fully account for why some truths endure while others fade. He emphasizes the necessity of fidelity, but he cannot explain what sustains fidelity over time. A revolution collapses. A new mathematical system is eventually replaced. A rupture in artistic form eventually becomes convention. But the Resurrection does not fade. It does not dissolve into historical change. It continues to summon subjects, continues to create fidelity across centuries and cultures, not as an abstraction but as an active, personal reality.

Badiou sees truth as subtraction—a militant rejection of the previous world. But what if truth is not simply a negation? What if an Event does not merely expose the void in the given order but fills it? What if truth is not merely something that breaks into history but something that sustains history itself?

This is the question Badiou cannot answer. His thought brings us to the threshold of the impossible, but it cannot step beyond it. His philosophy can recognize the radical rupture of Paul's encounter, but it cannot admit that Paul did not simply recognize an Event—he encountered a living presence.

To understand why the Resurrection is more than an Event, why it does not merely create fidelity but sustains it, we must push beyond Badiou's materialism. We must move from rupture to transfiguration.

The Resurrection as the Impossible Event

If Badiou's concept of the Event is a rupture that retroactively reconfigures what is possible, then the Resurrection represents something that exceeds even this model. It is not simply an irruption within history; it is the redefinition of history itself. If every Event, in Badiou's terms, exposes the contingency of a given situation, then the Resurrection reveals something even more staggering: that being itself is contingent upon love.

Here, Badiou's materialism reaches its absolute limit. He can acknowledge that the Resurrection functions as an Event for Paul—that it shattered his previous coordinates of meaning, producing in him an entirely new subjectivity. But Badiou cannot admit that the Resurrection is ontologically real, that it is not merely a subjective transformation but a cosmic upheaval. This is where his philosophical framework collapses under the weight of what it cannot contain.

Žižek attempts to resolve this tension by arguing that the Resurrection should be understood as a *symbolic* Event that reveals the revolutionary potential within the material world itself. But this merely displaces the problem. The disciples' transformation cannot be reduced to a symbolic awakening—their encounter with the risen Christ was, in their insistence, irreducibly physical. As N. T. Wright emphasizes, they were not proclaiming a spiritual truth but a material fact: the tomb was empty, and they had eaten with the risen Lord.[56]

Badiou (for his part) can account for political, mathematical, and even artistic ruptures, but he cannot account for what the Gospels present in stark simplicity: the body is gone. The guards fall as if dead, the women flee in terror, the disciples are bewildered. The empty tomb is not merely an absence; it is an excess that breaks the entire Symbolic Order. If we were to follow Badiou's framework, we would expect the Resurrection to be an interpretive act by the disciples, a militant declaration of new truth in the face of despair. But the accounts give us something far stranger. The disciples do not boldly proclaim a new reality at first—they are shattered, confused, afraid. They do not invent an Event; they encounter one, and it takes them time to even comprehend it.

What, exactly, is happening here? The guards "became like dead men" (Matt 28:4), while the dead man is alive. This is not merely a disruption of knowledge—it is a reversal of death itself. Badiou might say that the Resurrection belongs to the order of myth, an attempt to name the unnameable rupture. But this explanation does not hold. The disciples do not treat the Resurrection as a symbol or a metaphor. They do not proclaim that Jesus has spiritually risen in their hearts. They insist, against all expectation and at the cost of their lives, that he has physically risen.

Badiou's model of fidelity to the Event requires constant subjective commitment. Truth must be sustained by human effort, or else it vanishes. But what if the Resurrection is not simply an Event that demands fidelity, but an Event that sustains fidelity itself? What if the risen Christ is not merely an absent signifier but an active presence, continuing to draw people into a new mode of being?

Here, Badiou's entire structure begins to unravel. He assumes that all Events eventually lose their disruptive force, that truth procedures must constantly work against entropy to remain alive. But the Resurrection is different. It does not fade into historical memory, nor does it require an unbroken line of revolutionary militants to uphold its truth. It is not simply maintained; it remains active, continually generating new subjects, not through human willpower, but through divine initiative.

Jean-Luc Marion offers a striking contrast to Badiou here. If Badiou's Event disrupts the given order but requires human fidelity to sustain it, Marion presents a radically different vision: a phenomenon so excessive, so irreducible, that it does not depend on the subject's recognition at all. The Resurrection, in this light, is not an Event that needs to be maintained—it is a givenness that overwhelms human capacity to either uphold or negate it. Marion's concept of the saturated phenomenon describes precisely this kind of occurrence: an experience that is too full, too dense with presence, to be fully received. The Resurrection is not just a moment that reorients thought; it is a phenomenon that reconfigures being itself.[57]

༺༻

Badiou might call Paul the first militant of the Resurrection, the first to declare fidelity to the impossible. But Paul does not see himself as the architect of a new truth. He is not the one holding up the Event—he is held up by it. "By the grace of God I am what I am" (1 Cor 15:10). Badiou can speak of faithfulness, but he cannot speak of grace—of a truth that is not merely maintained by the subject but that actively calls, sustains, and transforms the subject.

This points to a fundamental limitation in modern philosophical materialism. Thinkers like Quentin Meillassoux have attempted to ground contingency itself as absolute, arguing that anything might happen—even the emergence of God.[58] But the Resurrection suggests something more radical: not that anything might happen, but that everything that happens is grounded in a love that precedes being itself. This is why Badiou's ontology of the void, powerful as it is, cannot fully account for the Event that transforms the void itself into a site of new creation.

Badiou's entire system relies on subtraction. The Event breaks with the previous situation; the subject remains faithful to this break, subtracting themselves from the old world. But the Resurrection does not merely subtract—it transforms. It does not merely break history; it remakes history. This is where Badiou's philosophy reaches its vanishing point. He can recognize rupture, but he cannot recognize new creation. He can understand commitment, but he cannot understand grace.

The Resurrection is not merely the introduction of a new possibility into history—it is the revelation that history itself was structured toward this impossible Event all along. The stone was always going to be rolled away. Death was always going to be undone. The foundation of reality was never merely being—it was always love stronger than death.

If every Event demands fidelity, the Resurrection demands something more: participation in a new order of existence. It is not merely a truth to be upheld but a life to be entered into. The empty tomb is not just an opening in history but an opening in being itself—a portal through which the world is being made new.

Badiou has brought us to the threshold of this mystery. But at the threshold, he must stop. His philosophy cannot go further. But we can.

The Void That Exceeds the Void

At the heart of Badiou's philosophy lies the concept of the void—the uncountable excess within any given situation, the absence that allows for rupture, the gap that an Event exposes and forces into recognition. But the Resurrection does something more than reveal a void within history or thought. It does not simply name an absence or bring the uncounted into view. Instead, it reveals that the void itself has been undone. The absence is not merely named—it is filled.

This is where Badiou's framework collapses under its own weight. For him, truth emerges when a subject declares fidelity to an Event that has reconfigured the structure of knowledge. But what happens when the Event is not just a break in the Symbolic Order, but the transformation of being itself? What happens when an Event does not just demand fidelity but draws all of reality into itself, refusing to be contained by any historical moment?

Badiou can understand the Cross—the rupture, the crisis, the subtraction from the world. But he cannot understand the empty tomb. The Cross still fits within his model of radical negation; it is a refusal, a scandal, a breaking of structures. But the Resurrection is not a negation—it is an impossible excess. It is not simply the emergence of a new political or ethical order. It is the reconfiguration of existence itself, an Event that does not rely on militant fidelity to sustain it but instead sustains those who encounter it.

Badiou's thought operates through subtraction—the Event as the refusal of the given world, the break that cannot be assimilated.

But the Resurrection is not just a subtraction. It is an addition, an overflowing, a gift. It is not merely an Event within history; it is the Event that remakes history from within. Badiou's model assumes that the subject remains faithful to the truth it has recognized, holding onto it despite the pressures of the world. But the Resurrection is not something to be merely held onto—it is something that holds.

Here, we must introduce a different challenge to Badiou's framework—one that does not emerge from the logic of negation but from the overwhelming presence of an encounter. Badiou's Events are mute; they require subjects to declare them into existence. But the Resurrection is already a declaration, already a summons. When Mary Magdalene encounters the risen Christ, she does not name the Event—she is named by it. "Mary," Jesus says (John 20:16), and in that moment, she is reconstituted. The void is not just exposed; it is filled with presence.

Marion's critique of philosophical materialism, as I have already intimated, is simple but devastating. Materialism, like that of Badiou, assumes that knowledge and truth emerge from an encounter with lack, with what remains unseen, uncounted, absent. But what if reality is not fundamentally structured by absence but by excess? What if the deepest truth of existence is not a void waiting to be ruptured, but a fullness so overwhelming that it cannot be reduced to any system of representation? In *Being Given*, Marion argues that true phenomena—what he calls saturated phenomena—do not submit to human conceptual grasping; they exceed it. They arrive not as gaps in the Symbolic Order but as a presence so radical that it cannot be domesticated.

The Resurrection is precisely such a phenomenon. It does not merely break history; it fills it. It is not just an interruption—it is the presence of a reality that the world cannot absorb, cannot contain, cannot master. The Gospel accounts do not depict the disciples interpreting an empty tomb as a sign to construct new meaning. Instead, the tomb is a wound in reality itself, an impossible presence that forces itself upon them. The risen Christ is not an idea to be grasped; he is given—in encounter, in speech, in touch, in breaking bread. The Event does not require their fidelity to sustain itself. It calls them into being. It creates them.

This reversal—from naming to being named—points to something deeper than just a shift in agency. It suggests what Jean-Louis Chrétien calls "the unforgettable and the unhoped for"—an Event that precedes and exceeds our capacity to recognize it.[59] The disciples don't discover the empty tomb; they are discovered by it. They don't interpret the Event; they are interpreted by it. This is what distinguishes the Resurrection from every other rupture in history: it is not just an irruption of the new, but the revelation of what was always already true.

☙

All of Badiou's thought, in the end, is an attempt to navigate the problem of finitude. The Event ruptures history, but it does not undo the finality of death itself. Even the most radical political rupture must contend with time, decay, and the eventual fading of its militant truth. This is why Badiou can speak of the Cross as a powerful moment of rupture, but he cannot allow for the Resurrection to be real—because if it is real, then death itself is no longer the last word. And if death is no longer the last word, then all of Badiou's categories must be rewritten. Reality is not structured by absence but by presence. Not by subtraction but by a fullness that cannot be exhausted.

We see this limitation of materialist thought in contemporary discussions of transhumanism and artificial intelligence—attempts to overcome death through technological means. But these efforts remain within the logic of subtraction and addition, trying to extend life rather than transform its very meaning. The Resurrection offers something radically different: not the prolonging of finite existence, but its fundamental transfiguration.

This is why the Eastern Christian tradition speaks of the Resurrection as the "eighth day" of creation—not simply another day in the sequence, but the day that transforms all other days. As Marion suggests, the Resurrection reveals that time itself was always oriented toward saturation, that the material world was always pregnant with divine possibility. What appeared as void was actually fullness waiting to be revealed.

This is where Badiou must stop. His philosophy can take us to the edge of the void, but it cannot cross over. It can reveal the absence at the heart of things, but it cannot account for an absence that has already been transformed into presence. His logic can bring us to the tomb, but it cannot allow the stone to be rolled away.

So we stand here, at the threshold of Badiou's system, and ask: What if the Event that reconfigures reality is not one we choose but one that has already chosen us?

What if the truth is not something we sustain, but something that sustains us?

What if the Resurrection is not merely the uncounted element appearing within the situation, but the fulfillment of reality's deepest structure, the truth toward which all other truths were already gesturing?

Badiou cannot answer these questions. But we can. And perhaps, if we allow the full weight of this impossible Event to take hold, we will finally recognize that the void was never empty at all.

Chapter Five

Already After the End

Agamben

It is an image that should not exist.

A young man lies dying, his body skeletal, his skin stretched paper thin over the architecture of his bones. His eyes—half open, unfocused—are fixed on something we cannot see. His lips part slightly, caught between speech and silence, as if even breath itself has become too great a labor. His father, heavyset in a flannel shirt, grips his son's hand with the desperate tenderness of someone holding on to the already half vanished. His mother and sister lean in from either side, their faces twisted—not with performative grief, but with the raw, unspeakable pain of witnessing, in real time, a beloved body turn into a corpse.

In another context, this could be a pietà. The broken son, the grieving mother, the looming father—Renaissance compositions, hands open in sorrow and acceptance. But there is no Michelangelo here, no gold leaf, no celestial light. The backdrop is not a cathedral but a sterile hospital room, its fluorescence unyielding. The wounds are not from Roman nails, but from the slow violence of disease, a body consumed from the inside out. And unlike the Christ figures that adorn churches, this image was not painted in veneration. It was captured by a journalist—then repurposed into a fashion advertisement.

Already After the End

The photographer, Therese Frare, took the image in 1990, as David Kirby lay dying of AIDS in an Ohio hospital. When Benetton ran it in 1992, they stripped it of context, history, particularity. No slogans, no branding, no message beyond the image itself. Just this—death, grief, exposure. It became one of the most controversial advertisements of all time, not because it revealed something unseen, but because it forced people to look at what they had already been trained to ignore. It was not just a photograph; it was a wound, printed on glossy paper, slipped between perfume ads and haute couture spreads.

The image echoes another from our time: Alan Kurdi, the three-year-old Syrian refugee, his tiny body washed up on a Turkish beach in 2015. Like the Benetton ad, this image too became a kind of global wound—reproduced endlessly, debated endlessly, yet somehow never fully processed. Both images expose what Giorgio Agamben means by "bare life": human existence stripped of political protection, reduced to pure biological vulnerability.[60] Both reveal bodies abandoned by the law, left to die while the world watches.

What are we seeing when we look at these images? A private moment, made public. A body, stripped of dignity yet turned into a symbol. A life at the threshold of death, its final moments transformed into an object of collective contemplation. This is bare life. This is sovereignty's failure.

The AIDS crisis was not merely a medical catastrophe; it was a political event. The state decided whose deaths would matter and whose would be allowed to pass in silence. Susan Sontag, writing in *AIDS and Its Metaphors*, saw how the disease became more than an illness—it became a judgment, a mark of exclusion, a way to separate the protected from the abandoned. Governments dragged their feet, denied funding, turned a blind eye to the suffering of those deemed marginal—gay men, sex workers, IV drug users. In a thousand different ways, power revealed its logic: some lives are grievable, others are not. Some bodies belong within the sphere of protection; others are left outside.

CRUX

This same logic is at work in Lars von Trier's *Dancer in the Dark* (2000), where Björk plays an immigrant worker slowly going blind, saving money for her son's operation. The film lays bare how the law does not simply fail to protect certain lives—it actively consigns them to death through bureaucratic inertia. Not through overt force, but through the slow violence of neglect, delay, administrative indifference. Sovereignty is not merely about enforcement; it is about the power to abandon.

And so we return to the image.

A body, neither fully alive nor fully gone. A death, neither public nor private. A spectacle, yet a silence. A man, neither inside nor outside the law. This is the space of *homo sacer*—the life that can be killed but not sacrificed, the body that exists at the threshold of sovereignty, included only in its exclusion.

Modern society believed it had abolished the logic of sacred violence, moved beyond the scapegoat, transcended the need for sacrificial victims. But the body in this photograph reveals the truth: we have not eliminated *homo sacer*—we have only bureaucratized him. As Jacques Derrida wrote in "Force of Law," the violence of law does not disappear in modern democracy—it becomes more subtle, more pervasive, more difficult to name.

This is where Giorgio Agamben begins. This is the horror he forces us to see. Not the spectacle of suffering itself, but the realization that this suffering is not incidental. It is structured. It is law. It is the system functioning exactly as designed. "The tradition of the oppressed," Walter Benjamin wrote in "Theses on the Philosophy of History," "teaches us that the 'state of emergency' in which we live is not the exception but the rule."[61] Agamben takes this further: the exception is not a temporary suspension of law—it is law's deepest truth.

To understand Agamben, we must first grasp this: the greatest power of the state is not its ability to enforce law, but its ability to suspend it. To create spaces where the law is inoperative, where the excluded remain caught between life and death, presence and absence. Where sovereignty manifests not in its application of justice, but in its decision on who will be abandoned.

And so, let us follow Agamben. Let us enter the space where law and life dissolve, where power and abandonment are indistinguishable. Let us look directly at what we were never meant to see.

Sovereignty, Law, and the Time That Remains

Giorgio Agamben is not a philosopher of abstractions. His work does not theorize in the void or produce elegant but inert conceptual machinery. Rather, it functions as an act of unmasking—a relentless exposure of the hidden structures that define reality, especially in moments of crisis.

Born in Italy in 1942, during the collapse of fascism, Agamben's intellectual formation was shaped by the realization that law does not simply uphold justice—it also legitimizes exclusion, violence, and abandonment. He studied under Martin Heidegger, absorbed Walter Benjamin's revolutionary insights, grappled with Carl Schmitt's theories of sovereignty, and engaged Michel Foucault's analysis of biopolitics. Yet his work is not merely a synthesis of these thinkers—it is an escalation, a final push toward the devastating realization that sovereignty, law, and exclusion form a single, inescapable mechanism.

Consider Kazuo Ishiguro's *The Unconsoled*, where Ryder finds himself trapped in a city governed by indecipherable rules and impossible obligations. He is simultaneously treated as an honored guest and subjected to escalating demands, never fully understanding the criteria by which he is judged. The novel captures something fundamental about Agamben's view of law—not as a system of justice, but as a machinery of capture that functions through its own opacity, keeping its subjects in a state of perpetual uncertainty.

For Agamben, sovereignty is not merely the power to rule; it is the ability to structure time itself. Who is included in history? Who is erased? Who exists within the law's protection, and who is cast into the void of nonexistence? The sovereign does not just determine what is legal or illegal—it decides what is visible, possible, thinkable.

We see this logic at work in contemporary detention centers, where asylum seekers exist in a perpetual present—neither admitted nor expelled, neither protected nor abandoned. As one detainee in an Australian offshore facility wrote in 2018: "We do not live in time here. We exist in a void between yesterday and tomorrow."[62] This suspension of time is not a malfunction of the system—it is how sovereign power operates.

The influence of Walter Benjamin is crucial here, particularly his reading of Paul's concept of messianic time. Paul's phrase *ho nyn kairos*—the "now time"—is not merely a historical moment but an interruption of history itself, a rupture in the existing order. For Agamben, messianic time is not about waiting for a future redemption but about a radical transformation of the present. It is the moment when the structures of law and power are revealed as contingent—when sovereignty trembles because it has been exposed as neither natural nor necessary.

Benjamin's "Theses on the Philosophy of History" sharpens this insight. History, he argues, is not a continuous, progressive unfolding but a series of interruptions, shocks, and fractures. The task of the messianic figure is not to patiently await the fulfillment of history but to seize upon these ruptures—to recognize the hidden potential within moments of crisis.

We might think, once more, of Tarkovsky's *Stalker* (1979), where three men enter a mysterious "Zone" where normal laws no longer apply. The Zone is both dangerous and full of possibility—a space where established orders break down, revealing their contingency. Like Benjamin's messianic time, the Zone does not merely represent chaos; it is a space where the given order exposes itself as fragile, where new possibilities might emerge.

Agamben deepens this insight, arguing that the present is always pregnant with its own undoing. The refugee, the undocumented, the prisoner at Guantánamo—these figures do not exist outside of history. Rather, they reveal history's fundamental instability. As Vietnamese American novelist Ocean Vuong writes in

On Earth We're Briefly Gorgeous: "They say the body is a temple. But I was born in ruins, pieced together from broken gods."[63] His words capture perfectly how certain bodies are marked by power as existing outside time, outside protection.

This is the horror Agamben forces us to see: sovereignty is strongest when it excludes. The refugee, the undocumented, the detainee—these are not mere victims of political dysfunction. They are the necessary by-products of sovereignty's logic. To include, sovereignty must also exclude. Law is not merely applied; it is withheld. Justice is not merely administered; it is suspended.

For this reason, Agamben turns to Carl Schmitt's definition of sovereignty: the sovereign is "he who decides on the exception."[64] But Agamben takes this further. The exception is not an anomaly; it is the system's foundation. States of emergency, indefinite detentions, legal limbos—these are not breakdowns of the legal order. They are the order. The refugee, the exile, the body placed outside protection—these figures do not exist beyond sovereignty. They reveal its essence.

J. M. Coetzee's *Waiting for the Barbarians* exposes this mechanism through its depiction of a colonial outpost at the empire's edge. The Magistrate's gradual realization of how law operates through exclusion—creating "barbarians" precisely to justify its own violence—reveals sovereignty's fundamental logic. The empire's torture chambers exist not despite the law but as its hidden foundation. Violence becomes routine precisely in these spaces where law renders itself inoperative.

Perhaps the starkest depiction of this logic is found not in philosophy, but in film. Lars von Trier's *Dogville* (2003) offers an unbearable meditation on exclusion as power. The town in *Dogville* does not exercise authority through direct oppression. Instead, it defines its power by drawing a boundary—deciding who may be included and under what conditions. The protagonist, Grace, is granted refuge, but only provisionally. She is permitted to exist within the town only insofar as she remains an exception, subject to escalating conditions of subjugation. The moment she ceases to be useful, she is expelled with brutal efficiency. Her inclusion was always predicated on her exclusion.

What *Dogville* exposes cinematically, Agamben reveals in political reality. Sovereignty does not need to impose terror to function; it only needs to decide who does not count. To be abandoned is not merely to be oppressed—it is to exist in a space where the law no longer acknowledges your presence, where justice is nothing more than a ghostly pretense.

This is the space of messianic time—the moment of exposure, the rupture where sovereignty's illusion begins to collapse. Like the mysterious Zone in *Stalker*, it is a space where established orders reveal their contingency, where new possibilities might emerge from the breakdown of the system.

But what happens after that collapse? What happens when law has been rendered inoperative, when the very structures of power begin to unravel? That is where Agamben takes us next.

Homo Sacer: The Life That Can Be Killed but Not Sacrificed

Speaking of *homo sacer* means naming something obscene, something that should not exist yet persists at the heart of political life. In ancient Rome, to be declared *homo sacer* was to be expelled from legal protection, cast into a paradoxical state of exclusion. Such a person could be killed with impunity, yet not offered as a sacrifice. Theirs was a death without meaning, a killing that neither restored order nor ruptured it—a mere expulsion from the realm of the human.

Agamben saw in this figure not a relic of a bygone world but a structure that has never ceased to function—a category that modernity has not abolished, but perfected. The logic of sovereignty has always depended upon the ability to decide who counts as fully human and who does not. The power to govern is, at its core, the power to exclude. *Homo sacer* is not an anomaly of ancient law; it is the silent condition of modern power.

Throughout history, this mechanism of exclusion has taken many forms. Medieval Europe marked certain bodies as touchable only by executioners. Colonial powers declared indigenous peoples outside the protection of law. Modern states create zones where rights are suspended indefinitely. Each iteration reveals the same underlying structure: sovereignty operates by creating categories of life that can be eliminated without consequence.

Consider Primo Levi's description in *If This Is a Man* of the *Muselmänner* in Auschwitz—those prisoners reduced to such a state of devastation that they seemed to exist between life and death. Their fellow inmates avoided looking at them, as if their condition were contagious. The camp guards barely registered their existence. They embodied what Agamben means by *bare life*—human beings stripped of everything except mere biological existence, yet still living, still breathing, still forcing the world to confront their unbearable presence.

In our time, this logic manifests in the bureaucratic violence of immigration systems. Asylum seekers find themselves trapped in processing centers, their lives suspended in administrative limbo. Neither officially rejected nor truly accepted, they exist in perpetual waiting, where time itself seems to stop. A report from a detention facility in Texas describes how detainees lose track of days, weeks, even months. Their watches are confiscated upon entry. The fluorescent lights never dim. Linear time dissolves into an endless present of waiting.[65]

Yet the condition of *homo sacer* extends beyond explicit detention. Look at how certain populations are marked as simultaneously essential and expendable. During the COVID-19 pandemic, workers in meat processing plants were declared "essential" yet denied basic protections. Their labor was necessary, but their lives were disposable. In Amazon warehouses, algorithms track workers' every movement, reducing human beings to units of productivity that can be discarded when they fail to meet automated standards. Modern sovereignty no longer needs explicit laws of exclusion—it operates through the cold logic of optimization and efficiency.

CRUX

Hanif Kureishi's *The Body* explores this commodification of life through a dystopian lens—a world where consciousness can be transferred to new bodies, but only for those who can afford it. The novel reveals how modern biotechnology creates new categories of *homo sacer*, new ways of marking certain bodies as available for use without genuine protection. The promises of technological transcendence mask an ancient logic of exclusion: some lives matter, others are mere raw material.

Agamben reminds us that this mechanism is already written into the foundation of Western political thought. The distinction between *zoē* (biological life) and *bios* (political life) has haunted philosophy since Aristotle. Not all lives are granted the full dignity of political existence. Some remain suspended in the category of mere life, their existence tolerated but never affirmed. This distinction has only grown more absolute as the modern state has refined its techniques of exclusion. The camps, the detention centers, the borderlands—these are not breakdowns of the legal order. They are its truest expression.

Gospel narratives illuminate this mechanism with devastating clarity. When the chief priests bring Jesus before Pilate, they do not ask for justice. They ask for a removal. "It is expedient that one man should die for the people, rather than the whole nation perish" (John 11:50). Expedience—not justice—is the logic of sovereignty. The machinery of law does not break down in the Passion narrative; it functions exactly as designed. Christ is expelled, not as a criminal, but as a figure outside the order itself—the one who must be abandoned so that order may remain intact.

But the Cross does something unprecedented. It reveals what has been hidden since the foundation of the world. If the scapegoat is innocent, then what does that say about the system that condemned him? What happens when the sovereign act of exclusion is no longer seen as justice, but as murder? The Gospel does not merely present Christ as an execution victim—it unmasks the very logic of sovereignty itself.

Jean-Luc Marion provides an additional challenge to Agamben's framework. If the political world is structured by the logic of exclusion, then where does love fit? Marion's concept of the saturated phenomenon, as I have already mentioned, presents an alternative: reality is not fundamentally structured by negation, but by overwhelming, irreducible presence. The sovereign may create zones of abandonment, but love refuses exclusion. The Resurrection, in this light, is not simply an overturning of death—it is the inbreaking of a reality in which exclusion is no longer possible.

Such recognition poses urgent questions: If Christ is *homo sacer*, then what does it mean to follow him? What does it mean to inhabit the space of the abandoned, to enter into solidarity with those whose existence has been deemed politically irrelevant? What does it mean to live in a world where sovereignty continues to function by deciding who will not count?

These are not theoretical questions. They define the world we already live in. And nowhere is this clearer than in the condition of the refugee, the one whose existence most fully reveals that sovereignty is nothing more than the ability to exclude.

The Refugee Crisis: Sovereignty's Spectral Failure

Across the Mediterranean, ghost ships drift—empty vessels stripped of navigation equipment, set on autopilot toward European shores. Human cargo—men, women, children fleeing war and poverty—packed into holds never meant for human bodies. Smugglers abandon ship miles from land, leaving their passengers to the mercy of currents and coast guards. These phantom vessels embody what Giorgio Agamben wrote about refugees as those who exist at the limits of the political order—"always only partially included in the legal system."[66] They are not simply exiles or migrants; they are figures that expose the fundamental contradiction of sovereignty: the power to include always depends on the power to exclude.

A refugee is not just someone without a home, but someone without a place in the law itself—someone whose very existence proves that the state cannot account for all life within its borders. Lebanese French author Amin Maalouf captures this liminal state in *Origins*: "To be a refugee means to learn a thousand unwritten rules, to speak without saying too much, to live knowing you are only provisionally tolerated."[67] His words echo through detention centers and refugee camps worldwide, where existence itself becomes provisional, contingent, always under threat of revocation.

Nowhere is this clearer than in offshore processing centers. On Nauru, on Christmas Island, in facilities deliberately placed beyond mainland jurisdiction, time operates differently. Mohsin Hamid's *Exit West* imagines magical doors that transport refugees between countries, but the reality is more devastating: spaces where people are neither fully admitted nor fully rejected, trapped in what one detainee called "the permanent temporary."[68] A 2024 investigation found asylum seekers held in these liminal spaces for over four years—caught in a system that neither formally recognizes nor expels them. One man, speaking from an encampment on the Texas border, described his experience: "I am not waiting for an answer anymore. There is no answer."[69]

Vietnamese filmmaker Trinh T. Minh-ha's *Forgetting Vietnam* (2015) reveals another dimension of displacement—how certain bodies become perpetually foreign even in their own land. Her camera lingers on faces caught between presence and absence, belonging and exile. These are not just aesthetic choices; they expose how sovereignty operates by creating zones of indistinction, spaces where the line between inclusion and exclusion is deliberately blurred.

The refugee condition is not a temporary crisis—it is the structural foundation of the modern nation-state. For Agamben, the camp is not an aberration; it is the paradigm of political power. The legal limbo of the refugee does not represent a failure of governance but rather its purest expression. To rule, the state must not only define who belongs but must also decide who is left to exist in a state of perpetual uncertainty.

Consider how this mechanism plays out in seemingly mundane settings. In airport detention rooms, in temporary holding facilities, in the bureaucratic maze of asylum applications, time itself begins to collapse. The structures that organize life—work, citizenship, family, legal recognition—disintegrate into indefinite waiting. Jenny Erpenbeck's *Go, Went, Gone* follows retired classics professor Richard as he encounters African refugees in Berlin. Through his eyes, we see how the system doesn't simply exclude; it creates a particular kind of existence—visible only as a problem to be managed, a crisis to be contained.

Along the US-Mexico border, this logic reveals itself with brutal clarity. In 2025, the Department of Homeland Security intensified its campaign of indefinite detention and strategic expulsion. Responding to mounting political pressure, they transferred migrants with criminal backgrounds to offshore holding facilities. Families were split across different states, asylum seekers forced into years of bureaucratic paralysis. The logic was clear: sovereignty does not need to resolve the crisis. It only needs to make the crisis permanent.

The ability to exclude is the hidden foundation of sovereignty. When a government builds detention centers rather than pathways to asylum, when it refuses to process visas but increases deportation quotas, when it creates the legally invisible but economically essential workforce of the undocumented—it is not failing. It is working exactly as designed. As philosopher Catherine Malabou notes in *The New Wounded*, certain forms of violence don't destroy identity—they create new ones, shaped precisely by their exclusion from normal protections.[70]

Massive databases track movement across borders. Biometric systems catalog faces, fingerprints, iris patterns. Artificial intelligence algorithms assess "risk factors" and "threat levels." Yet this technological sophistication serves an ancient function: to determine who may exist within the law's protection and who must remain outside it. Contemporary surveillance doesn't solve the refugee crisis—it perfects the mechanisms of exclusion.

The nation-state defines itself against the refugee, just as the law defines itself against those it abandons. This is why Agamben names the refugee the central figure of modernity—not only because of their suffering but because their very existence reveals the mechanisms of exclusion that states depend on but refuse to acknowledge. Valeria Luiselli's *Tell Me How It Ends* structures itself around the forty questions asked of undocumented children in immigration court. Each question reveals how the system's apparent concern for legal process masks its true function: to maintain the power to exclude.

A system that produces endless exclusion is a system that has already collapsed. We do not live in a world where sovereignty is being challenged; we live in a world where sovereignty has already unraveled, but refuses to admit its own undoing. To recognize this is to finally understand that the refugee crisis is not an exception. It is the rule.

Katargein: The Cross as the Unraveling of Law

Speaking of Christ as the end of the law is not metaphor. Paul, in Rom 10:4, declares with stunning directness: "For Christ is the end [*telos*] of the law, so that there may be righteousness for everyone who believes." The Greek *telos* does not merely mean conclusion— it signifies fulfillment, completion, exhaustion. Agamben seizes upon *katargein*, a term Paul uses again and again, meaning not to abolish, but to render inoperative. The Cross does not destroy the law—it exposes its contingency, its fragility, its powerlessness before what it cannot control.

Flannery O'Connor's *The Violent Bear It Away* captures something of this unraveling through its young protagonist's desperate struggle against grace. The more fiercely he tries to escape his calling, the more completely law and order collapse around him. His resistance doesn't lead to simple rebellion but to a more profound undoing—what O'Connor calls "the action of grace in territory held largely by the devil."[71] This is not mere lawlessness; it is law encountering what it cannot contain.

Law does not govern by simple enforcement. Its true function emerges in its capacity to suspend itself. Sovereignty is most fully realized when it declares that law does not apply. The camp, the refugee center, the detention facility—these are not failures of the legal system but its fullest expressions, spaces where law exists only as the possibility of its own suspension. Consider how this plays out in contemporary legal proceedings. In 2024, a federal judge ruled that certain detained asylum seekers had "no enforceable rights" under US law, while simultaneously acknowledging their presence within US jurisdiction.[72] The contradiction is not a flaw—it is precisely how the system functions.

Pilate's judgment exemplifies this paradox: "I find no fault in him, yet I deliver him unto you." Authority does not operate on a principle of justice but on the ability to withhold justice at will. To rule is not to uphold the law but to decide when it ceases to function. László Nemes's *Son of Saul* (2016) reveals this mechanism with devastating clarity through its protagonist, a *Sonderkommando* in Auschwitz forced to assist in the camp's operations. The law that should protect life becomes the very mechanism of its destruction, yet continues to function precisely through its own suspension.

The Passion thus stands as more than a theological event—it signifies a crisis for sovereignty itself. The trial of Christ is a non-trial. Pilate, representative of Rome, does not uphold the law but evades it. He performs authority while exposing its absence. "What is truth?" he asks, and does not wait for an answer (John 18:38). Legal authority collapses into its opposite, revealing that governance is not the administration of justice but the ability to decide who will be abandoned.

This unraveling of law is also a central theme in modern dystopian literature, where authority sustains itself not by enforcing legal norms, but by creating an opaque, shifting order that traps its subjects. In Kafka's *The Trial*, perhaps the most famous example in all of literature, Josef K. is arrested and prosecuted without ever knowing his crime, caught in a bureaucratic nightmare where judgment is both omnipresent and inscrutable. Here, law does not protect or govern—it ensnares, ensuring its subjects remain within its grasp without the possibility of resolution.

Katargein follows this logic. The Cross is not merely an act of suffering; it marks the moment when law's performance of order collapses into its opposite. Contemporary philosopher Catherine Mills, in *The Philosophy of Agamben*, suggests that this collapse reveals something crucial: governance does not create justice; it determines who will be cast out.[73] In this unraveling, the illusion of sovereignty stands exposed.

Romanian filmmaker Cristian Mungiu's *Beyond the Hills* (2012) stages this unraveling in a remote Orthodox monastery, where attempts to maintain religious and legal order spiral into violence. The more rigidly the characters try to apply the law, the more completely it undoes itself. This is not simply a criticism of religious authority—it reveals how any system based on law's absolute claims contains the seeds of its own dissolution.

What does it mean to live beyond such a collapse? Agamben presses the question to its most unbearable conclusion. If sovereignty has already exhausted itself, why does the world continue as if it has not? The answer unsettles. The catastrophe is not impending—it has already happened. Don DeLillo's *The Silence* imagines a world where digital systems suddenly stop working, but the real horror isn't the breakdown—it's how people continue performing their usual routines as if nothing has changed. This is precisely Agamben's point about law: its collapse has already occurred, yet we maintain its gestures, its rituals, its claims to authority.

Recognition of this reality carries profound consequences. Political life, built upon the mechanics of exclusion, sustains itself by refusing to acknowledge its own demise. To see the Cross clearly is to recognize that sovereignty has already failed, persisting only because its death remains unspoken. As poet Christian

Wiman writes in *My Bright Abyss*: "What we call doubt is often simply dullness of mind and spirit, not the absence of faith at all, but faith latent with fatigue and fear."[74]

Paul does not merely announce the end of the law but calls his listeners into a new way of being: "The old has passed away, behold, the new has come" (2 Cor 5:17). Yet this renewal does not restore stability. It ushers in a condition where the logic of exclusion no longer applies. The *katargein* of the law is not just an event to be understood—it is an existential rupture. To follow Christ is to live as if the world that still pretends to govern has already collapsed.

And yet, sovereignty lingers. Like a ghost, like a law already nullified but still obeyed. The unraveling has happened, but the world has not yet realized it. We stand in the aftermath of a revelation we refuse to see.

The Catastrophe: Sovereignty Has Already Been Undone

No turning back remains possible. The unraveling has already happened. Law, sovereignty, the fragile architecture of inclusion and exclusion—these were never solid structures, only temporary performances of control, and now the performance is breaking down. What was once hidden now stands in the open, no longer masked by legal fictions. And yet, the world refuses to see it.

David Kirby lay on his deathbed, skeletal, hands clutched in his father's grasp. A man still alive, yet already positioned for death, a body that did not belong in the world of the living but had not yet passed into the silence of the dead. The photograph of his final moments, first a private grief, then a national image, then an advertisement, was transformed into something else entirely: a spectacle of bare life. And like all spectacles, it revealed what could not be spoken outright. He was neither inside nor outside, neither fully abandoned nor fully protected. This was not just a photograph of a dying man. It was a photograph of a world order that had already come undone.

CRUX

Béla Tarr's final film, *The Turin Horse* (2011), offers a vision of this aftermath. For two and a half hours, we watch a father and daughter perform the same tasks day after day as their world slowly dims. The wind never stops howling. The light grows weaker. Their routines become more futile. Yet they continue, as if nothing has changed, as if maintaining the gestures of normal life could ward off the reality that their world has already ended. This is where we are now—performing the motions of a system that has lost its foundation, maintaining the fiction of sovereignty even as it dissolves.

This is where Agamben takes us. The refugee who waits, the prisoner detained indefinitely, the migrant trapped in a legal limbo that stretches not for months but for years—these are not temporary states of emergency. They are the condition of our world. They do not stand at the edges of political life. They *are* political life. They are the proof that law no longer functions as law, that sovereignty no longer governs but simply decides, arbitrarily, who will be allowed to exist.

"For the present form of this world is passing away," Paul writes in 1 Cor 7:31, and the words land now with a new kind of force. Not a prophecy, not a future event, but a recognition: the world as we know it is already dissolving. Law still stands, yet its foundations are gone. The categories remain, but their content is empty. The performance continues, but there is no longer a stage beneath it. Like characters in a Beckett play, we go through the motions of a drama whose meaning has evaporated, speaking lines we no longer believe in.

What does it mean to live in a world that no longer believes in itself? What does it mean to inhabit a sovereignty that has already collapsed but refuses to admit its own undoing? László Krasznahorkai's *The Melancholy of Resistance* presents a town awaiting a mysterious circus that brings only destruction. The horror isn't in the destruction itself, but in how the townspeople maintain their normal routines even as everything falls apart. They continue to respect authorities that have already lost their power, to follow laws that have already lost their force.

One sees this in the paintings of Francis Bacon—the human form twisted, caught in grotesque spasms, trapped in the space of a failed gesture. A mouth open in a scream, but no voice emerges. The body is still there, but its integrity has already come apart. Bacon's figures do not simply suffer; they reveal something more disturbing—the inability to recognize when death has already arrived.

And yet, the true horror is not that sovereignty has collapsed. The true horror is that it remains, not as governance, not as justice, but as a spectral force, haunting a world that has already moved beyond it. Sovereignty, no longer able to rule, lingers as pure decision, pure exclusion, a mechanism that exists only to abandon. In words commonly attributed to Pinchas Gutter, we traverse our days while remaining outside them, spectators of our own acts, survivors of our own experiences.

This is the space in which Christ dies. His execution is not a scandal just because he is innocent—it is a scandal because it reveals that law has never been anything more than the arbitrary power to cast out. Pilate's judgment is not a misfire of justice. It is the perfect realization of what sovereignty always was: a structure that does not need reasons, only decisions. "I find no fault in him," he says, and yet hands him over to be crucified. The judgment contains its own nullification, yet proceeds anyway—the pure form of law revealed in the moment of its complete emptiness.

If the Cross unmasks this structure, then the Resurrection does not simply offer hope—it forces a confrontation. If Christ has risen, then what does that say about the structures that condemned him? If sovereignty could not hold him, then why do we continue to obey its ghost? Derek Jarman's *Blue* (1993), created as the filmmaker was going blind from AIDS-related complications, consists of a single blue screen for its entire duration, with only sound and narration—images deliberately withheld, as if to say that some realities can no longer be represented, only shown through their absence. We have reached such a moment in political life.

This is where the catastrophe takes on its final form. The unraveling of sovereignty does not merely mean the failure of a political order. It means that the world we have taken for granted—the world of law, of nations, of governance—has already ceased to function. The refugee is not an exception. The law does not fail in moments of crisis. *The law is the crisis.* As poet Anne Carson writes in *Decreation*, we find ourselves returned to the beginning—but to a beginning we have never actually experienced before.[75]

And yet the world continues, as if it were not already undone. Contemporary Mexican author Yuri Herrera's *Kingdom Cons* presents a society where power operates purely through spectacle, where law has become nothing but performance—yet everyone continues to act as if the performance still holds meaning. This is not simply hypocrisy or delusion. It is the condition of living after the end, of continuing to perform sovereignty even when we know it has lost its foundation.

There is no final act of destruction. No spectacular collapse. No decisive break between the old world and the new. Only the realization, creeping and inescapable, that we are already living after the end. That sovereignty has already been unmade. That the state does not govern. That the categories we use to organize the world—citizen and stranger, legal and illegal, inside and outside—are as empty as Pilate's basin, as hollow as the tomb that could not hold him.

To follow Christ in this world is not to hope for sovereignty's end. It is to live as if it has already ended. The catastrophe is not coming. We are already in it. The only question that remains is whether we will finally open our eyes to see it.

Conclusion
Eating God (At the End of Time)

I.

THERE IS A MOMENT before everything changes. Before the act is committed. Before the threshold is crossed. It is the moment of hesitation, of hesitation's unbearable weight, when one realizes that after this—after taking, after eating—there will be no return to what came before.

The first time I read Georges Bataille, I felt something shift in me. It was not like encountering a philosopher. It was more like standing at the edge of a cliff and feeling the pull of the drop. Bataille was not a thinker who offered solutions; he was one who pushed everything to the breaking point—himself, language, meaning. His writings on sacrifice, on eroticism, on the sacred, all circled the same unbearable reality: that true communion, true exposure, true participation in something beyond the self, demands nothing less than dissolution. One cannot hold oneself back from it. One must cross the threshold completely—or not at all.

And then there was Laure.

Colette Peignot, known as Laure, was more than Bataille's companion—she was his match, the one who was willing to take everything further than he could. She understood something he only theorized: that the breaking open he sought was not an idea but an Event, something that had to happen in the flesh. She believed that true communion could take place only in complete exposure. To speak truly to another is to destroy oneself, to become nothing but an opening, a wound through which everything flows.

For Bataille and Laure, communion meant undoing, meant offering oneself in total vulnerability. It was an experiment in what Bataille would later call sovereignty—a state beyond preservation, beyond utility, beyond the logic of survival itself. But the experiment was doomed. Laure's body broke before she could reach the state of pure communication she sought. She died in 1938, her illness consuming her, and Bataille was left with nothing but the wound of her absence. Their communion, as raw and real as it was, remained enclosed within finitude. It could not break free from death. It could not persist.

What if they were right? What if communion is only real when it is absolute? When it is total exposure, without remainder? When one holds nothing back? And if that is true, then what does it mean that Christianity—the faith of incarnation, of God-made-flesh—offers a communion where one does not merely offer oneself, but consumes?

Bataille and Laure reached toward a truth they could not fully grasp: that if communion is real, it must be more than an act of self-giving—it must be something that remains.

II.

Wounds that destroy, wounds that gather. The difference contains everything. When Bataille and Laure tried to communicate through mutual destruction, they discovered something real: that genuine communion requires rupture, requires exposure beyond what safety can allow. But their experiment remained trapped in the logic of annihilation. Their wounds could only burn out, could only consume. The very intensity that promised transcendence led to dissolution. Nothing remained but absence, but loss, but the endless circling of what could not be preserved.

Yet something in their failed experiment gestured toward a deeper truth—one they glimpsed but could not grasp. The need for complete exposure, the desire to be seen even in one's most

Conclusion

unbearable state, the hunger for communion beyond the boundaries of the self—all of this pointed toward something that exceeds both secular reason and conventional piety. What if the wound itself could become not just a site of destruction but a space of dwelling?

This is what Thomas understood, though not at first. "Unless I put my finger into the mark of the nails, and put my hand into his side, I will not believe" (John 20:25). The demand seems almost violent in its physicality—not to see from a distance, not to contemplate or theorize, but to enter the wounds themselves. And Christ's response is even more striking. He does not heal the wounds, does not close them, does not transform them into mere signs of what has passed. Instead, he preserves them, presents them, offers them as places of encounter: "Put your finger here and see my hands, and bring your hand and put it into my side" (John 20:27).

The wounds remain open. Even after Resurrection, even in his glorified body, Christ keeps these ruptures, these openings, these places where divinity has been torn open to human touch. And for centuries, those wounds have been seen not merely as evidence of suffering but as spaces into which we are invited to enter.

Bernard of Clairvaux saw this. Amid the theological storms of the twelfth century, inside a small monastic cell, he wrote of the dove making her nest in the clefts of the rock, resting within the wounds of Christ. "Place me like a seal over your heart, like a seal on your arm" (Song 8:6). These ruptures in divine flesh became dwelling places, caves carved into the rock of God's own body. What appeared as devastation reveals itself as sanctuary. The wounds do not close but remain as spaces that can be entered, inhabited, lived within.

Julian of Norwich saw this in the horror of the plague. As the Black Death devoured entire cities, she remained enclosed in her cell, watching through a small window as the world collapsed. In the midst of this catastrophe, she received visions of Christ's wounds that transformed everything. These were not merely displays of past suffering. They became fountains, wellsprings, sources from which divine life poured into present devastation. Even as bodies failed and social order collapsed, these wounds remained open—not as memories of past trauma but as current channels of presence. "The wounds of Christ are wide enough to hold all humanity."[76]

Paul understood this at the most intimate level. He does not speak of wounds as an idea, but as something that marks him physically: "I bear in my body the marks of Jesus" (Gal 6:17). The Greek word he uses—*stigmata*—suggests something inscribed in flesh, branded into being. His wounds from persecution, his scars from stoning, his body broken by imprisonment—these become points of participation in divine wounding. "I am filling up what is lacking in Christ's afflictions" (Col 1:24). Not because Christ's suffering was insufficient, but because it continues to open itself to new suffering, continues to make space within its own ruptures for all human pain to enter.

Where Bataille and Laure's wounds could only destroy, these wounds gather. They do not close. They do not heal. They remain as permanent openings in the flesh of reality itself, making space for what human exposure alone could never sustain.

High on Mount La Verna, in the autumn of 1224, this mystery took physical form. The wounds that Francis received were not symbols, not imitations, not even mystical experiences in the ordinary sense. They were actual openings in flesh, points where divine and human substance met and mingled. For two years, Francis bore these stigmata—not as signs pointing to some other reality but as real portals where heaven and earth bled into each other. The wounds had to be bandaged. Blood stained his habit. Pain was constant. And yet, those who saw them reported something impossible: light pouring through the ruptures, as if these gaps in human flesh had become windows into divine life.

Something extraordinary happened to Bridget of Sweden—not just a vision but a revelation that transformed how wounds could be understood. Where others saw five wounds in Christ's body, she saw thousands—5,480 to be exact. This was not poetic exaggeration but visceral reality, each wound counted, each one real. Divine flesh mapped with pain, every surface opened. Yet these countless wounds did not diminish into metaphor. Each one remained a potential space of encounter, a place where human suffering could enter into contact with divine presence. The multiplicity of wounds revealed something crucial: that Christ's body is not just personally but cosmically wounded, opened not just in one place but everywhere, gathering all devastation into itself.

And now, in Gaza, these wounds open again. Not metaphorically, not symbolically, but as real ruptures in the fabric of the world.

This is not just suffering. *It is a stigmata.*

III.

The Holy Family Catholic Church stands in Gaza City, its stone walls battered but unbroken. The Mass continues. It should not, and yet it does. There is no food left. No water. The air is thick with smoke, with grief, with the unspoken knowledge that not everyone who was here yesterday is here today. But the priest lifts the Host, and the people gather. There is no choir. There is no incense. Only the murmuring of prayers, the rustling of bodies shifting, kneeling, standing. And yet, presence remains.

Here, in Gaza, in a church where the walls tremble with each distant detonation, the words are spoken again:

> *Hoc est enim corpus meum.*
> *This is my body.*

What does it mean to speak these words in a place where bodies are torn apart daily? To call something flesh when flesh is what has been most brutally reduced to nothing? To say that this bread is real presence when presence itself is fragile, flickering, under siege?

The hands that lift the Host are dirty. The people who receive it are starving. And yet, something happens here that philosophy cannot grasp—something that refuses the logic of absence, refuses the inevitability of destruction. The Mass should not continue. And yet, it does.

CRUX

What is this presence that does not retreat, even in devastation?
The Host is lifted, the ruins tremble, and still—Christ remains.

IV.

There is a moment in John's Gospel that remains, even now, incomprehensible to me.

It is not the crucifixion—not the nails, not the spear, not the moment Christ breathes his last. It is before all that, in the sixth chapter, when Christ speaks of eating his flesh and drinking his blood. The scandal here is not just about transgression or taboo—it is about something that exceeds our very categories of inside and outside, self and other, presence and absence.

The crowd listens, then recoils. Not because they do not understand, but because they do. This is what Žižek would call "the traumatic Real"—not confusion, but clarity so intense it cannot be integrated into normal consciousness.

This is not poetry. This is not metaphor. This is something else entirely—"the saturated phenomenon," an experience that overwhelms our capacity to conceptualize it.

They murmur against him. "How can this man give us his flesh to eat?" (John 6:52). Some are confused. Others are disgusted. Many turn away. But Christ does not soften his words. He does not explain them away. He does not correct them or offer gentler phrasing. Instead, he presses further, intensifying rather than resolving the scandal.

"Unless you eat the flesh of the Son of Man and drink his blood, you have no life in you" (John 6:53). The words land with full force. The crowd fractures. Many leave. It is too much. Like Lacan's analysands confronting the Real, they retreat from what they cannot symbolize.

And yet, he does not call them back. He does not offer an easier path. He simply watches them go. This is the moment everything turns. What Christ is saying is not *come and understand*. It is not *come and believe*. It is *come and consume*. It is the last thing

Conclusion

anyone expects. It is the last thing anyone can make sense of. And yet, it is the only thing that matters.

Abide in me, and I in you. (John 15:4)

⁊⁕

To eat God is to cross a threshold from which there is no return. The Eucharist is not a symbol. It is not a reenactment. It is not an act of remembrance. It is consumption.

And consumption is never neutral. It is not a passive act. To eat is to take something into oneself, to dissolve it, to let it enter into one's very substance. But here, what is eaten does not dissolve. What is taken in does not cease to be. The Eucharist is not digested. It abides.

This is why John 6 is so unbearable. Why the crowd recoiled. Why many left. They understood what was being said, and they understood it too well. *Unless you eat the flesh of the Son of Man and drink his blood, you have no life in you.* The words were not misunderstood. They were intolerable.

To eat God is to surrender autonomy. It is to allow divinity to enter not just the soul, but the gut, the bloodstream, the cells. It is intimacy beyond safety. It is union beyond consent.

And yet, the command is given: *Take. Eat.*

The terror of this demand has been softened over centuries. Wrapped in gilded vessels. Made polite with ritual. But the first Christians knew what was being asked. The Romans did not misinterpret the Eucharist as cannibalism—they saw it for what it was. A scandal. A breaking of every boundary between the human and the divine, the eater and the eaten.

And so the question remains: Who can bear to eat this?

In Gaza, the Eucharist is received by mouths that have not tasted bread in days. The Body of Christ enters bodies that have been hollowed out by hunger, by grief, by waiting. The Host dissolves, but Christ does not disappear. He does not retreat. He remains.

This is not a meal. This is a rupture.

The act has been committed. The threshold has been crossed. And there is no return.

V.

But what does it mean to cross this threshold? What does it mean for Christ not just to be eaten, but to remain?

Abide in me, and I in you. These words shatter the normal categories of religious discourse. Here we find not mere devotion, not obedience, not even worship. Something else emerges—something terrifying in its physicality, radical in its implications.

Throughout centuries, theologians have tried to make it more palatable, more acceptable. Yet the words resist domestication. The claim remains raw, disturbing, absolute.

Consider the progression: He does not say, *Follow me.* He does not say, *Think of me.* He does not say, *Imitate me.* Instead—with shocking directness—he says, *Eat me.* This is what Lacan might call "the Real of Christianity"—the point where symbolic mediation fails completely.

But then comes something even stranger: *Abide in me, and I in you.* Here the very structure of subjectivity begins to fold in on itself. No longer can we maintain clear distinctions between inside and outside, between consumer and consumed. Like a Möbius strip—where inside and outside exist in continuous flow—the boundaries between Christ and believer become impossible to locate.

Within this mutual indwelling, the Eucharist reveals itself as more than consumption. It is not simply Christ entering us. It is not merely divine presence taken into human flesh. Instead, we encounter what the Eastern Church calls *perichoresis*—an infinite exchange, a reciprocal interpenetration of divine and human life. As Maximus the Confessor wrote: "God and man are paradigms of one another, that as much as God is humanized to man through love for mankind, so much is man able to be deified to God through love."[77]

Conclusion

Radically, this exchange dissolves our normal metaphysics of presence and absence. The Eucharist operates like a quantum state where particles can exist in multiple positions simultaneously. We are in Christ; Christ is in us. These are not sequential events but a single reality that exceeds spatial logic. As Jean-Luc Nancy suggests in *Corpus*, we encounter here a body that is neither present nor absent, neither internal nor external, neither spiritual nor material in the usual sense.

Deep implications unfold. If we take this mutual indwelling seriously, then salvation itself must be reconceived. No longer is it about ascending to God or God descending to us. Instead, we find ourselves caught up in what Balthasar calls "the trinitarian circulation of divine life."[78] The boundaries between divine and human become permeable—not erased, but transformed into sites of endless exchange.

Bataille glimpsed something of this in his theory of communication through wounds, but even he stopped short of its full implications. He saw the rupture, the breaking open, but not where it leads. He recognized the necessity of dissolution but could not conceive of a dissolution that creates rather than destroys. The Cross opens this wound in being itself, but the Eucharist reveals it as a permanent condition—not a trauma to be healed but a space of perpetual exchange.

VI.

The stories have been told. Now comes the weight of what they mean.

Bataille and Laure sought communion in wounds, exposing themselves to each other in a way that refused to be mediated by symbols or images. Like Lacan's Real, they reached for something beyond the Symbolic Order, beyond the illusions of ego and identity. They believed that real encounter required something that exceeded language, exceeded recognition, exceeded even the structures of subjectivity itself. But their story ended in dissolution. The very intensity that made their communion possible also made it unsustainable. As Lacan might say, they touched the Real, but could not survive its trauma.

And now, in Gaza, the same pattern emerges in a different register. The Mass is still being said, but it too exists beyond explanation. Like Agamben's *homo sacer*, it operates in a space of exception—not governed by normal rules of power or sovereignty. It does not function within the logic of politics or law. It does not restore order. It does not lift anyone out of suffering. It does not prevent the next missile from falling. And yet, it is real in a way that exceeds both symbolization and raw materiality.

What we witness here is what Badiou would call an Event—a moment when something impossible breaks into the order of being. But unlike the political Events that Badiou typically analyzes, this rupture does not announce a new truth so much as it reveals an old one made viscerally present: that divine love manifests most fully in the spaces of absolute abandonment. This is not theological theory—it is phenomenological fact, happening in real time among the rubble.

Bataille's error was in thinking that exposure alone could bring redemption—that to be stripped of illusion was enough. Like Žižek's reading of the death of God, he saw the necessity of negation but missed its strange afterlife. The question that haunts his work, that he could never fully answer, is this: What is communion if it does not persist? What is encounter if it does not remain? Laure died. The world continued. The wounds were real, but they did not hold. They did not gather anything into themselves. They did not draw anything beyond their own moment of rupture.

But what happens when communion is not just between two? What happens when the wound itself is not just suffered, but shared? When it does not dissolve, but endures? This is where Girard's insights about sacred violence must be pushed further: What if the wound does not close, but instead becomes the site of a new life? What if, as Marion suggests in *God Without Being*, absence itself becomes the mode of presence?

The Eucharist does not function like Bataille's tearing apart (or what he sometimes calls "déchirement"). It does not remain

Conclusion

isolated, two bodies suffering separately, touching for only a moment before vanishing. The Eucharist is not a brief exposure—it is an abiding. This is what sets it apart from every other form of communion, every other attempt at radical encounter. Christ's broken body is not a transient spectacle; it is a presence that gathers, a wound that does not seal, a body that remains open.

It is what Lacan might call "the Thing" but transformed into gift, what Žižek terms "the sublime object" but made edible, what Badiou names "the Event" but rendered persistent.

In Gaza, that same presence lingers. It does not undo suffering—that would be too simple, too much like magic or escape. Instead, it does something far stranger, something that none of our theoretical frameworks quite capture: it insists on remaining within suffering itself. This is not the sublation of dialectics, not the transformation of negative into positive. It is closer to what Simone Weil called *decreation*—a presence that manifests through its own emptying, a strength that appears as weakness, a gathering that happens through dispersal.

And now we begin again. We shift from what has been broken toward what still holds, toward what remains. This remaining is not preservation or protection. It is not the maintenance of boundaries or the assertion of identity. It is something else entirely—a mode of presence that operates through absence, a form of communion that happens precisely where communion seems impossible.

VII.

This is why traditional metaphysics fails to capture what happens in the Eucharist. We require a new ontology altogether—one that can think mutual indwelling without reducing it to simple unity or maintaining absolute separation. As Catherine Pickstock argues in *After Writing*, the Eucharist demands "a liturgical metaphysics" where being itself is reconceived as gift and return, as endless circulation rather than static presence.

The Eucharist emerges as not merely an Event that passes but an enduring state—a permanent rupture in the fabric of reality itself. Like Badiou's Event, it breaks with the normal order of being, but unlike his conception of the Event, it does not simply inaugurate a new truth—it establishes a new mode of existence altogether. The Body of Christ is taken into us, dissolves, yet does not disappear. It remains, not as an object we possess or a substance we contain, but as a reality that possesses and contains us even as we possess and contain it.

This is not the temporary communion that Bataille sought, not the momentary fusion of mystic experience, not even the profound but passing connection of human love. It does not burn out like the failed experiments of human communion—the way Laure left Bataille, the way all lovers eventually leave, the way all wounds eventually heal over and vanish. Instead, it establishes a permanent circulation, an eternal exchange that transforms both the divine and human participants without dissolving their distinction.

This is where we begin to grasp the radical difference between human attempts at communion and what happens in the Eucharist. Bataille reached for a communion that could not hold because he conceived of it purely in terms of mutual destruction—two subjects breaking themselves open before each other until nothing remained. But the Eucharist, by contrast, holds precisely because it is not simply given but taken up into an ongoing exchange. Christ's Body does not dissolve into oblivion; it is gathered into those who receive him. And in turn, those who receive him are gathered into something greater than themselves—not by losing their identity but by finding it transformed within this infinite circulation. It is not simply a love that tears open, but a love that remains open, that establishes a permanent wound which becomes not a site of trauma but a space of endless exchange.

This is what John of Damascus meant when he wrote that in the Eucharist, "we both deify and are deified."[79] The exchange goes both ways—not that we become God or God becomes merely human, but that a new kind of existence emerges, one in which divine and human life enter into perpetual circulation. This is why Maximus the Confessor could claim that Christ's Body in the Eucharist is the site where the very distinction between time and eternity becomes porous—that the reception of Christ's flesh initiates us into a mode of life where finite being is continually suspended within infinite transformation.

Consider how this transforms our understanding of what it means to consume and be consumed. In normal eating, we take something external and make it part of ourselves through a process of destruction and absorption. The food ceases to be what it was and becomes part of our own flesh. But in the Eucharist, this logic is reversed and complexified. We consume Christ's Body, yes, but in doing so we are consumed by it. We take it in, but it takes us in. The very act of consumption becomes an act of being consumed, not in the sense of destruction but in the sense of being drawn into a larger life.

This is what the church fathers meant by *theosis*—not that we become God in some pantheistic sense, but that we are drawn into the very life of God while remaining ourselves, caught up in what Gregory of Nyssa called *the eternal progress into divine life*, an infinite growth that never reaches its end because its end is infinite. The Eucharist does not collapse the difference between God and humanity; it renders the difference itself dynamic. It does not dissolve us into the divine but pulls us into an unceasing transformation. It is a rupture, yes, but a rupture that does not end—an Event that does not pass into history but remains as an ongoing movement, an opening that cannot be closed.

And this is why, at the center of all things, the Eucharist remains a wound that does not close. It is not a doctrine to be understood, not a mystery to be solved, but an encounter that undoes the one who receives it. It is rupture, circulation, transformation. It is where presence and absence collapse into each other, where time and eternity bleed together, where the boundaries between God and man, self and other, consumption and being consumed, are broken open and made new.

VIII.

Everything we have traced—the wounds that do not close, the Eucharist that consumes and is consumed, the perichoretic circulation that refuses to resolve—has been leading here. To the final question. To the final rupture.

All things are being gathered. This is the promise. This is the vision. But what does it mean for all things to be gathered? And into what? A final resolution? A grand reconciliation? A moment where the contradictions cease, where suffering is undone, where the wounds are finally healed? This is what we long for. This is what Teilhard de Chardin glimpsed when he spoke of the Omega Point, when he described the Mass on the World. He saw the final consummation, the moment when all of creation—every molecule, every star, every broken fragment of history—would be gathered into the Body of Christ, transformed in the radiance of divine presence. He saw the world itself become Eucharist.[80]

It is beautiful. It is terrifying. And I do not see it.

I can dare to hope, but I do not see it. What I see is this: the contradiction that will not resolve. The wound that remains open. The body given, broken, eaten. The irreducible strangeness of a kingdom that does not conquer but submits, a power that refuses worldly strength. The unresolvable, unbearable scandal that does not end. The world does not look like it is moving toward transfiguration. It looks like it is unraveling. The wounds remain. The violence does not cease. And yet, the Eucharist continues. The Mass is still said, still breaking into the wreckage of history, still gathering what cannot be gathered.

> *He is before all things, and in him all things hold together.*
> (Col 1:17)

Teilhard saw a world being drawn upward, toward completion. But the Cross does not point upward. It is driven into the earth. It is planted in suffering, in failure, in death. It does not ascend; it descends. And the Eucharist follows it, into the ruins, into the hunger, into the mouths of those who do not know if they will

Conclusion

eat again. The world is not moving smoothly toward its completion. It is groaning under its own weight. And yet, the Eucharist abides.

> And I, when I am lifted up from the earth, will draw all people to myself. (John 12:32)

Teilhard spoke of evolution's trajectory toward God, of a process moving toward completion, toward final unity. But Christ does not gather like gravity pulling all things into itself. He gathers as the Crucified, as the one who remains wounded. He gathers through brokenness, through fragmentation, through a body that is given and eaten but never exhausted. The Eucharist is not a smooth progression into wholeness. It is a rupture that never stops rupturing.

The Mass continues in places of devastation. It continues in Gaza, in churches with broken walls, in hands still reaching for bread when there is no bread left. It continues in the hollowed-out bodies of the starving, in the whispered prayers of the displaced, in the ruins where it should not still be spoken, but is. The hands that lift the Host are unsteady, caked in dust, and yet the words are said again: *Hoc est enim corpus meum.* This is my body. And the contradiction deepens. Because these words should not make sense in a world still so torn apart, and yet they remain.

The Eucharist does not erase the Cross. It does not undo suffering. It does not close the wound of history. It enters it. It abides in it. It is the body, broken and given, endlessly. And if all things are being gathered into Christ, they are not being gathered into wholeness. They are being gathered into this: into the wound that does not close, into the love that does not leave, into the presence that does not retreat even when the world is collapsing.

> *For in him all the fullness of God was pleased to dwell, and through him to reconcile to himself all things, whether on earth or in heaven, making peace by the blood of his cross.* (Col 1:19–20)

This is the final contradiction. The world remains at the crux. At the contradiction. At the rupture that does not heal. It is not ascending into unity, into clarity, into some final harmonious reconciliation. It is being drawn into Christ. And Christ remains crucified.

Teilhard was right to say that all things are being gathered. But it is not a smooth ascent. It is not a grand, unbroken movement toward light. It is a gathering into wounds. It is the drawing in of all things into suffering that does not dissolve but remains, that does not end but abides. The world does not become whole. It becomes Eucharist. And the Eucharist is the wound of God laid open for all.

This is where it ends. Not in resolution. Not in peace. Not in a synthesis that makes everything whole.

But in the only place it can end.

In the scandal of the Cross.

Endnotes

Chapter One: Love's Impossible Gift: Lacan

1. Lacan's claim that "the unconscious is structured like a language" is developed throughout "Function and Field of Speech." See also Lacan, "Discourse to Catholics," 14.
2. Lacan, "Function and Field of Speech."
3. Lacan, *Encore*.
4. Lacan, "Mirror Stage as Formative."
5. Celan, *Poems of Paul Celan*, 153.
6. Augustine, *Confessions* 1.1.
7. Lacan, *Psychoses*, 31–40.
8. Hölderlin, *Some Poems of Hölderlin*, 22.
9. Blanchot, *Writing of the Disaster*, 7.
10. Lacan, *Four Fundamental Concepts of Psychoanalysis*, 72.
11. Balthasar, *Action*, 336.
12. Julian of Norwich, *Revelations of Divine Love*, ch. 8.
13. Lacan, *Transference*, 34; also see Lacan's seminar 12 (unpublished).
14. For Lacan's discussion of love, see Lacan, *Transference*; and Fink, *Lacan on Love*.
15. Nancy, "Shattered Love," 98.
16. Duras, *Hiroshima Mon Amour*.
17. Bataille, *Erotism*, 11.
18. Bachmann, *Darkness Spoken*, 12–13.
19. Valente, *Fragmentos de un libro futuro*, 91.
20. Žižek, *Puppet and the Dwarf*, 6.

Chapter Two: Faith Against Itself: Žižek

21. Cave, "Conversations with Nick Cave."
22. Žižek, *Puppet and the Dwarf*, 53.
23. Lynch, *Christ and Apollo*, 19–24.
24. James Smith, *How (Not) to Be Secular.*
25. Christian Smith, *Soul Searching*, 162–63.
26. Žižek, *On Belief*, 12.
27. Gregory of Nyssa, *Life of Moses* 2.163.
28. Eckhart, *Complete Mystical Works*, 422.
29. Balthasar, *Mysterium Paschale*, 89.
30. Žižek, *On Belief*, 145–51.
31. Žižek, *Puppet and the Dwarf*, 59–91.
32. Žižek, "Fear of Four Words."
33. Weil, *Gravity and Grace*, 109.
34. Žižek, *Puppet and the Dwarf.*
35. Williams, *On Christian Theology*, 186.
36. Žižek, *Puppet and the Dwarf*, 171.
37. Žižek, *Living in the End Times*, 110.
38. Romero, *Voice of the Voiceless*, 114.
39. See Rother, *Shepherd Cannot Run.*

Chapter Three: The Unbearable Spectacle: Girard

40. Girard, *Violence and the Sacred*, 4.
41. Girard, *Things Hidden*, 25–26.
42. Girard, *Violence and the Sacred*, 79.
43. Girard, *Things Hidden*, 166.
44. Balthasar, *Mysterium Paschale*, 89.
45. Balthasar, *Action.*
46. Posselt, *Edith Stein*, 191.
47. Girard, *Things Hidden*, 271.
48. Zahn, *In Solitary Witness*, 54.
49. Nagai, *Bells of Nagasaki*, 107.
50. Nagai, *Bells of Nagasaki*, 118.
51. Glynn, *Song for Nagasaki*, 168.

Chapter Four: Breaking the Void: Badiou

52. See Badiou, *Being and Event.*
53. See Badiou, *Theory of the Subject.*
54. See Milbank, *Future of Love.*
55. Merton, *Conjectures of a Guilty Bystander*, 158.

Endnotes

56. Wright, *Resurrection of the Son of God*, 685–710.
57. See Marion, *Being Given*.
58. See Meillassoux, *After Finitude*.
59. Chrétien, *Unforgettable and Unhoped For*, 128.

Chapter Five: Already After the End: Agamben

60. See Agamben, *Homo Sacer*.
61. Benjamin, "Theses on the Philosophy of History," thesis 8.
62. Boochani, *No Friend but the Mountains*, 128.
63. Vuong, *On Earth We're Briefly Gorgeous*, 137.
64. Schmitt, *Political Theology*, 5.
65. McCullough, "Hundreds of Migrants."
66. Agamben, *Homo Sacer*, 28.
67. Maalouf, *Origins*, 213.
68. Hamid, *Exit West*, 98.
69. Levin, "What the US Asylum Process Is Really Like."
70. Malabou, *New Wounded*, 121–41.
71. See O'Connor, "Nature and Aim of Fiction."
72. Department of State v. Muñoz, 599 U.S. 899 (2024).
73. Mills, *Philosophy of Agamben*, 59–79.
74. Wiman, *My Bright Abyss*, 102.
75. Carson, "Every Exit Is an Entrance," 185.

Conclusion: Eating God (At the End of Time)

76. See Julian of Norwich, *Revelations of Divine Love*, 22.
77. Maximus the Confessor, "Difficulty 10," 109.
78. Balthasar, *Mysterium Paschale*, 77.
79. John of Damascus, "Exact Exposition of the Orthodox Faith" 4.13.
80. Teilhard de Chardin, "Mass on the World."

Suggested Reading

Chapter One: Love's Impossible Gift: Lacan

1. Fink, Bruce. *The Lacanian Subject: Between Language and Jouissance*. Princeton, NJ: Princeton University Press, 1997.
2. Evans, Dylan. *An Introductory Dictionary of Lacanian Psychoanalysis*. London: Routledge, 1996.
3. Homer, Sean. *Jacques Lacan*. Routledge Critical Thinkers. London: Routledge, 2005.
4. Nobus, Dany. *Jacques Lacan and the Freudian Practice of Psychoanalysis*. Makers of Modern Psychotherapy. London: Routledge, 2000.
5. Chiesa, Lorenzo. *Subjectivity and Otherness: A Philosophical Reading of Lacan*. Short Circuits. Cambridge, MA: MIT Press, 2007.
6. Hook, Derek. *Six Moments in Lacan: Communication and Identification in Psychology and Psychoanalysis*. London: Routledge, 2017.
7. Verhaeghe, Paul. *Does the Woman Exist? From Freud's Hysteric to Lacan's Feminine*. New York: Other, 1999.
8. Van Haute, Philippe. *Against Adaptation: Lacan's "Subversion" of the Subject*. New York: Other, 2002.

9. Roudinesco, Elisabeth. *Jacques Lacan: An Outline of a Life and a History of a System of Thought*. Cambridge, UK: Polity, 1999.
10. Žižek, Slavoj. *Looking Awry: An Introduction to Jacques Lacan Through Popular Culture*. October Books. Cambridge, MA: MIT Press, 1992.
11. Thurston, Luke. *Re-Inventing the Symptom: Essays on the Final Lacan*. New York: Other, 2002.
12. Dor, Joël. *Introduction to the Reading of Lacan: The Unconscious Structured Like a Language*. New York: Other, 1998.

Chapter Two: Faith Against Itself: Žižek

1. Sharpe, Matthew, and Geoff M. Boucher. *Žižek and Politics: A Critical Introduction*. Edinburgh: Edinburgh University Press, 2010.
2. Myers, Tony. *Slavoj Žižek*. Routledge Critical Thinkers. London: Routledge, 2003.
3. Kotsko, Adam. *Žižek and Theology*. Philosophy and Theology. Edinburgh: T&T Clark, 2008.
4. Taylor, Astra, dir. *Examined Life: Philosophy in the Streets*. New York: Zeitgeist, 2008.
5. Pound, Marcus. *Theology, Psychoanalysis and Trauma*. Veritas. London: SCM, 2007.
6. Dean, Jodi. *Žižek's Politics*. London: Routledge, 2006.
7. Crockett, Clayton. *Interstices of the Sublime: Theology and Psychoanalytic Theory*. Perspectives in Continental Philosophy. New York: Fordham University Press, 2007.
8. Parker, Ian. *Slavoj Žižek: A Critical Introduction*. Las Vegas: Pluto, 2004.
9. Butler, Rex. *Slavoj Žižek: Live Theory*. London: Continuum, 2005.

Suggested Reading

10. Kay, Sarah. *Žižek: A Critical Introduction*. Cambridge, UK: Polity, 2003.
11. Fiennes, Sophie, dir. *The Pervert's Guide to Ideology*. New York: Zeitgeist, 2012.
12. Davis, Creston, et al., eds. *Theology and the Political: The New Debate*. Sic 5. Durham, NC: Duke University Press, 2005.

Chapter Three: The Unbearable Spectacle: Girard

1. Williams, James G. *The Girard Reader*. Spring Valley, NY: Crossroad, 1996.
2. Palaver, Wolfgang. *René Girard's Mimetic Theory*. Translated by Gabriel Borrud. Studies in Violence, Mimesis & Culture. East Lansing: Michigan State University Press, 2013.
3. Kirwan, Michael. *Discovering Girard*. Boston: Cowley, 2005.
4. Alison, James. *The Joy of Being Wrong: Original Sin Through Easter Eyes*. Spring Valley, NY: Crossroad, 1998.
5. Oughourlian, Jean-Michel. *The Genesis of Desire*. Translated by Eugene Webb. Studies in Violence, Mimesis, and Culture. East Lansing: Michigan State University Press, 2010.
6. Schwager, Raymund. *Must There Be Scapegoats? Violence and Redemption in the Bible*. New York: Harper & Row, 1987.
7. Warren, James. *Compassion or Apocalypse? A Comprehensible Guide to the Thought of René Girard*. New Alresford, UK: Christian Alternative, 2013.
8. Dumouchel, Paul, ed. *Violence and Truth: On the Work of René Girard*. Stanford, CA: Stanford University Press, 1988.
9. Hamerton-Kelly, Robert G. *Sacred Violence: Paul's Hermeneutic of the Cross*. Minneapolis: Fortress, 1992.
10. Fleming, Chris. *René Girard: Violence and Mimesis*. Cambridge, UK: Polity, 2004.

Suggested Reading

11. Grande, Per Bjørnar. *Mimesis and Desire: An Analysis of the Religious Nature of Mimesis and Desire in the Work of René Girard*. London: Lambert Academic, 2009.

12. Bailie, Gil. *Violence Unveiled: Humanity at the Crossroads*. Spring Valley, NY: Crossroad, 1995.

Chapter Four: Breaking the Void: Badiou

1. Hallward, Peter. *Badiou: A Subject to Truth*. Minneapolis: University of Minnesota Press, 2003.

2. Pluth, Ed. *Badiou: A Philosophy of the New*. Cambridge, UK: Polity, 2010.

3. Bartlett, A. J., and Justin Clemens, eds. *Alain Badiou: Key Concepts*. Durham, UK: Acumen, 2010.

4. Feltham, Oliver. *Alain Badiou: Live Theory*. London: Continuum, 2008.

5. Bosteels, Bruno. *Badiou and Politics*. Post-Contemporary Interventions. Durham, NC: Duke University Press, 2011.

6. Norris, Christopher. *Badiou's "Being and Event": A Reader's Guide*. London: Continuum, 2009.

7. Barker, Jason. *Alain Badiou: A Critical Introduction*. Las Vegas: Pluto, 2002.

8. Brassier, Ray. *Nihil Unbound: Enlightenment and Extinction*. New York: Palgrave Macmillan, 2007.

9. Toscano, Alberto. *The Theatre of Production: Philosophy and Individuation Between Kant and Deleuze*. Renewing Philosophy. New York: Palgrave Macmillan, 2006.

10. Gillespie, Sam. *The Mathematics of Novelty: Badiou's Minimalist Metaphysics*. Melbourne: Re.press, 2008.

Suggested Reading

11. Calcagno, Antonio. *Badiou and Derrida: Politics, Events and Their Time*. London: Continuum, 2007.

12. Corcoran, Steven. *The Badiou Dictionary*. Philosophical Dictionaries. Edinburgh: Edinburgh University Press, 2015.

Chapter Five: Already After the End: Agamben

1. Murray, Alex, and Jessica Whyte, eds. *The Agamben Dictionary*. Philosophical Dictionaries. Edinburgh: Edinburgh University Press, 2011.

2. Prozorov, Sergei. *Agamben and Politics: A Critical Introduction*. Thinking Politics 1. Edinburgh: Edinburgh University Press, 2014.

3. De la Durantaye, Leland. *Giorgio Agamben: A Critical Introduction*. Stanford, CA: Stanford University Press, 2009.

4. Dickinson, Colby. *Agamben and Theology*. Philosophy and Theology. Edinburgh: T&T Clark, 2011.

5. Norris, Andrew, ed. *Politics, Metaphysics, and Death: Essays on Giorgio Agamben's "Homo Sacer."* Durham, NC: Duke University Press, 2005.

6. Whyte, Jessica. *Catastrophe and Redemption: The Political Thought of Giorgio Agamben*. SUNY Series in Contemporary Continental Philosophy. New York: State University of New York Press, 2013.

7. Watkin, William. *The Literary Agamben: Adventures in Logopoiesis*. London: Continuum, 2010.

8. McLoughlin, Daniel. *Agamben and Radical Politics*. Critical Connections. Edinburgh: Edinburgh University Press, 2016.

9. Abbott, Mathew. *The Figure of This World: Agamben and the Question of Political Ontology*. Crosscurrents. Edinburgh: Edinburgh University Press, 2014.

SUGGESTED READING

10. Murray, Alex. *Giorgio Agamben*. Routledge Critical Thinkers London: Routledge, 2010.

11. Calarco, Matthew, and Steven DeCaroli, eds. *Giorgio Agamben: Sovereignty and Life*. Stanford, CA: Stanford University Press, 2007.

12. Zartaloudis, Thanos. *Giorgio Agamben: Power, Law and the Uses of Criticism*. Nomikoi: Critical Legal Thinkers. London: Routledge, 2010.

Conclusion: Eating God (At the End of Time)

1. Chauvet, Louis-Marie. *Symbol and Sacrament: A Sacramental Reinterpretation of Christian Existence*. Translated by Madeleine M. Beaumont and Patrick Madigan. Collegeville, MN: Liturgical, 1995.

2. Bynum, Caroline Walker. *Holy Feast and Holy Fast: The Religious Significance of Food to Medieval Women*. The New Historicism: Studies in Cultural Poetics 1. Berkeley: University of California Press, 1988.

3. Cavanaugh, William T. *Torture and Eucharist: Theology, Politics, and the Body of Christ*. Challenges in Contemporary Theology. Oxford: Blackwell, 1998.

4. Metz, Johann Baptist. *Faith in History and Society: Toward a Practical Fundamental Theology*. Translated by J. Matthew Ashley. Spring Valley, NY: Crossroad, 2007.

5. Schillebeeckx, Edward. *Christ the Sacrament of the Encounter with God*. London: Sheed and Ward, 1963.

6. Lubac, Henri de. *Corpus Mysticum: The Eucharist and the Church in the Middle Ages*. Translated by Gemma Simmonds. Faith in Reason: Philosophical Enquiries. Notre Dame, IN: University of Notre Dame Press, 2007.

Suggested Reading

7. Fagerberg, David W. *Theologia Prima: What Is Liturgical Theology?* Mundelein, IL: Hillenbrand, 2004.

8. Falque, Emmanuel. *The Metamorphosis of Finitude: An Essay on Birth and Resurrection*. Perspectives in Continental Philosophy. New York: Fordham University Press, 2012.

9. Irwin, Kevin W. *Models of the Eucharist*. Mahwah, NJ: Paulist, 2005.

10. Wood, Susan K. *One Baptism: Ecumenical Dimensions of the Doctrine of Baptism*. Collegeville, MN: Liturgical, 2009.

11. Morrill, Bruce T. *Anamnesis as Dangerous Memory: Political and Liturgical Theology in Dialogue*. Collegeville, MN: Liturgical, 2000.

12. Radcliffe, Timothy. *Why Go to Church? The Drama of the Eucharist*. London: Continuum, 2008.

Bibliography

Agamben, Giorgio. *Homo Sacer: Sovereign Power and Bare Life*. Translated by Daniel Heller-Roazen. Meridian: Crossing Aesthetics. Stanford: Stanford University Press, 1998.
Augustine. *Confessions*. Translated by Henry Chadwick. Oxford World's Classics. Oxford. Oxford University Press, 1991.
Bachmann, Ingeborg. *Darkness Spoken: The Collected Poems of Ingeborg Bachmann*. Translated by Peter Filkins. Brookline, MA: Zephyr, 2005.
Badiou, Alain. *Being and Event*. Translated by Oliver Feltham. London: Continuum, 2005.
———. *Theory of the Subject*. Translated by Bruno Bosteels. London: Continuum, 2009.
Balthasar, Hans Urs von. *The Action*. Translated by Graham Harrison. Vol. 4 of *Theo-Drama: Theological Dramatic Theory*. San Francisco: Ignatius, 1994.
———. *Mysterium Paschale: The Mystery of Easter*. Translated by Aidan Nichols. San Francisco: Ignatius, 2000.
Bataille, Georges. *Erotism: Death and Sensuality*. Translated by Mary Dalwood. San Francisco: City Lights, 1986.
Benjamin, Walter. "Theses on the Philosophy of History." In *Illuminations: Essays and Reflections*, edited by Hannah Arendt, translated by Harry Zohn, 253–64. New York: Schocken, 1969.
Blanchot, Maurice. *The Writing of the Disaster*. Translated by Ann Smock. Lincoln: University of Nebraska Press, 1995.
Boochani, Behrouz. *No Friend but the Mountains: Writing from Manus Prison*. Translated by Omid Tofighian. Sydney: Picador Australia, 2018.
Cage, John. *4'33"*. Musical composition. First performed by David Tudor at Woodstock, New York, August 29, 1952.
Carson, Anne. "Every Exit Is an Entrance (A Praise of Sleep)." In *Decreation: Poetry, Essays, Opera*, 181–94. New York: Knopf, 2005.
Cave, Nick. "Conversations with Nick Cave." Live Q&A at Barbican Centre, London, June 19, 2019.

BIBLIOGRAPHY

Celan, Paul. *Poems of Paul Celan.* Translated by Michael Hamburger. Rev. ed. New York: Persea, 2002.

Chrétien, Jean-Louis. *The Unforgettable and the Unhoped For.* Translated by Jeffrey Bloechl. Perspectives in Continental Philosophy. New York: Fordham University Press, 2002.

Coetzee, J. M. *Waiting for the Barbarians.* New York: Penguin, 1999.

DeLillo, Don. *The Silence.* New York: Scribner, 2020.

Denis, Claire, dir. *Trouble Every Day.* France: Rezo, 2001.

Department of State v. Muñoz, 599 U.S. 899 (2024).

Derrida, Jacques. "Force of Law: The 'Mystical Foundation of Authority.'" In *Acts of Religion,* edited by Gil Anidjar, translated by Mary Quaintance, 230–98. New York: Routledge, 2002.

Dreyer, Carl Theodor, dir. *Ordet.* Copenhagen: A/S Palladium, 1955.

Duras, Marguerite. *Hiroshima Mon Amour.* Translated by Richard Seaver. New York: Grove, 1961.

Eckhart, Meister. *The Complete Mystical Works of Meister Eckhart.* Translated by Maurice O'C. Walshe. New York: Crossroad, 2009.

Erpenbeck, Jenny. *Go, Went, Gone.* Translated by Susan Bernofsky. New York: New Directions, 2017.

Fink, Bruce. *Lacan on Love: An Exploration of Lacan's Seminar VIII, "Transference."* Cambridge, UK: Polity, 2015.

Girard, René. *Things Hidden Since the Foundation of the World.* Translated by Stephen Bann and Michael Metteer. Stanford: Stanford University Press, 1987.

———. *Violence and the Sacred.* Translated by Patrick Gregory. Baltimore: Johns Hopkins University Press, 1977.

Glynn, Paul. *A Song for Nagasaki: The Story of Takashi Nagai—Scientist, Convert, and Survivor of the Atomic Bomb.* San Francisco: Ignatius, 2009.

Gregory of Nyssa. *The Life of Moses.* Translated by Abraham J. Malherbe and Everett Ferguson. Classics of Western Spirituality. New York: Paulist, 1978.

Grünewald, Matthias. *Isenheim Altarpiece.* Ca. 1512–1516. Oil on panel. Musée Unterlinden, Colmar, France.

Hamid, Mohsin. *Exit West.* New York: Riverhead, 2017.

Heaney, Seamus. *The Cure at Troy: A Version of Sophocles' "Philoctetes."* New York: Farrar, Straus and Giroux, 1991.

Herrera, Yuri. *Kingdom Cons.* Translated by Lisa Dillman. Oakland: And Other Stories, 2017.

Herzog, Werner, dir. *Into the Abyss.* New York: IFC, 2011.

Hölderlin, Friedrich. *Some Poems of Hölderlin.* Translated by Frederic Prokosch. Norfolk, CT: New Directions, 1943.

Ishiguro, Kazuo. *The Unconsoled.* New York: Knopf, 1995.

Jarman, Derek, dir. *Blue.* London: Channel 4, 1993.

John of Damascus. "An Exact Exposition of the Orthodox Faith." Translated by E. W. Watson and L. Pullan. In *Nicene and Post-Nicene Fathers,* edited

BIBLIOGRAPHY

by Philip Schaff and Henry Wace, 2nd ser., 9:1–101. Peabody, MA: Hendrickson, 1994.

Julian of Norwich. *Revelations of Divine Love*. Edited by A. C. Spearing. Translated by Elizabeth Spearing. Penguin Classics. London: Penguin Classics, 1998.

Kafka, Franz. *The Trial*. Translated by Breon Mitchell. New York: Schocken, 1998.

Kapoor, Anish. *Void Field*. 1989. Sandstone and pigment. Originally exhibited at the XLIV Venice Biennale; now in the collection of the National Gallery of Australia, Canberra.

Kieślowski, Krzysztof, dir. *A Short Film About Killing* [*Krótki film o zabijaniu*]. Zespół Filmowy "Tor," 1988.

Krasznahorkai, László. *The Melancholy of Resistance*. Translated by George Szirtes. New York: New Directions, 1998.

Kureishi, Hanif. *The Body*. New York: Scribner, 2004.

Lacan, Jacques. "Discourse to Catholics." In *"The Triumph of Religion": Preceded by "Discourse to Catholics,"* translated by Bruce Fink, 3–54. Cambridge, UK: Polity, 2013.

———. *Encore, 1972–1973*. Edited by Jacques-Alain Miller. Translated by Bruce Fink. The Seminar of Jacques Lacan 20. New York: Norton, 1998.

———. *The Four Fundamental Concepts of Psychoanalysis*. Edited by Jacques-Alain Miller. Translated by Alan Sheridan. Rev. ed. The Seminar of Jacques Lacan 11. New York: Norton & Company, 1998.

———. "Function and Field of Speech and Language in Psychoanalysis." In *Écrits: A Selection*, translated by Bruce Fink, 197–268. New York: Norton, 2002.

———. "The Mirror Stage as Formative in the Function of the I as Revealed in Psychoanalytic Experience." In *Écrits: A Selection*, translated by Bruce Fink, 75–81. New York: Norton, 2006.

———. *The Psychoses, 1955–1956*. Edited by Jacques-Alain Miller. Translated by Russell Grigg. The Seminar of Jacques Lacan 3. New York: Norton, 1993.

———. *Transference*. Edited by Jacques-Alain Miller. Translated by Bruce Fink. The Seminar of Jacques Lacan 8. Cambridge, UK: Polity, 2015.

Levi, Primo. *If This Is a Man*. Translated by Stuart Woolf. New York: Orion, 1959.

Levin, Sam. "What the US Asylum Process Is Really Like, in Applicants' Own Words: 'I've Waited 10 Years.'" *Guardian*, June 4, 2024. https://www.theguardian.com/us-news/article/2024/jun/04/asylum-process-first-person-esssays.

Luiselli, Valeria. *Tell Me How It Ends: An Essay in Forty Questions*. Minneapolis: Coffee House, 2017.

Lynch, William F. *Christ and Apollo: The Dimensions of the Literary Imagination*. New York: Sheed and Ward, 1960.

Maalouf, Amin. *Origins: A Memoir*. Translated by Catherine Temerson. New York: Farrar, Straus and Giroux, 2008.

BIBLIOGRAPHY

Malabou, Catherine. *The New Wounded: From Neurosis to Brain Damage.* Translated by Steven Miller. Forms of Living. New York: Fordham University Press, 2012.

Mallarmé, Stéphane. "Un coup de dés jamais n'abolira le hasard" [A throw of the dice will never abolish chance]. *Nouvelle Revue Française* (July 1914) 24.

Marion, Jean-Luc. *Being Given: Toward a Phenomenology of Givenness.* Translated by Jeffrey L. Kosky. Cultural Memory in the Present. Stanford: Stanford University Press, 2002.

———. *God Without Being.* Translated by Thomas A. Carlson. Religion and Postmodernism. Chicago: University of Chicago Press, 1991.

Maximus the Confessor. "Difficulty 10." In *Maximus the Confessor*, edited and translated by Andrew Louth, 91–152. Early Church Fathers. London: Routledge, 1996.

McCullough, Jolie. "Hundreds of Migrants Arrested under Gov. Greg Abbott's Border Initiative Were Jailed for Weeks Without Charges, Lawyers." *Texas Tribune*, September 27, 2021. https://www.texastribune.org/2021/09/27/texas-border-migrants-jail/.

Meillassoux, Quentin. *After Finitude: An Essay on the Necessity of Contingency.* Translated by Ray Brassier. London: Continuum, 2008.

Merton, Thomas. *Conjectures of a Guilty Bystander.* New York: Doubleday, 1966.

Milbank, John. *The Future of Love: Essays in Political Theology.* Eugene, OR: Cascade, 2009.

Mills, Catherine. *The Philosophy of Agamben.* Continental European Philosophy. Montreal: McGill-Queen's University Press, 2008.

Minh-ha, Trinh T., dir. *Forgetting Vietnam.* Berkeley, CA: Moongift, 2015.

Mungiu, Cristian, dir. *Beyond the Hills.* Bucharest: Mobra, 2012.

Nagai, Takashi. *The Bells of Nagasaki.* Translated by William Johnston. Tokyo: Kodansha International, 1984.

Nancy, Jean-Luc. *Corpus.* Translated by Richard A. Rand. Perspectives in Continental Philosophy. New York: Fordham University Press, 2008.

———. "Shattered Love." In *The Inoperative Community*, edited by Peter Connor and translated by Peter Connor et al., 82–109. Theory and History of Literature 76. Minneapolis: University of Minnesota Press, 1991.

Nemes, László, dir. *Son of Saul.* Budapest: Mozinet, 2016.

O'Connor, Flannery. "The Nature and Aim of Fiction." In *Mystery and Manners: Occasional Prose*, edited by Sally Fitzgerald and Robert Fitzgerald, 63–86. FSG Classics. New York: Farrar, Straus & Giroux, 1969.

———. *The Violent Bear It Away.* FSG Classics. New York: Farrar, Straus and Giroux, 1960.

Pärt, Arvo. *Stabat Mater.* Composed 1985. ECM Records, 1992.

Pasolini, Pier Paolo, dir. *The Gospel According to St. Matthew* [*Il Vangelo secondo Matteo*]. Rome: Titanus, 1964.

BIBLIOGRAPHY

Pickstock, Catherine. *After Writing: On the Liturgical Consummation of Philosophy*. Challenges in Contemporary Theology. Oxford: Blackwell, 1998.
Posselt, Teresia Renata. *Edith Stein: The Life of a Philosopher and Carmelite*. Edited by Susanne M. Batzdorff et al. Rev. ed. Washington, DC: ICS, 2005.
Rahner, Karl. *Foundations of Christian Faith: An Introduction to the Idea of Christianity*. Translated by William V. Dych. New York: Crossroad, 1978.
Resnais, Alain, dir. *Hiroshima Mon Amour*. Paris: Cocinor, 1959.
Romero, Oscar. *Voice of the Voiceless: The Four Pastoral Letters and Other Statements*. Translated by Michael J. Walsh. Maryknoll, NY: Orbis, 1985.
Rother, Stanley. *The Shepherd Cannot Run: Letters of Stanley Rother, Missionary and Martyr*. Edited by George Rigazzi. Huntington, IN: Our Sunday Visitor, 2021.
Schmitt, Carl. *Political Theology: Four Chapters on the Concept of Sovereignty*. Translated by George Schwab. Chicago: University of Chicago Press, 2005.
Scorsese, Martin, dir. *Silence*. Los Angeles: Paramount, 2016.
Smith, Christian. *Soul Searching: The Religious and Spiritual Lives of American Teenagers*. With Melinda Lundquist Denton. Oxford: Oxford University Press, 2005.
Smith, James K. A. *How (Not) to Be Secular: Reading Charles Taylor*. Grand Rapids: Eerdmans, 2014.
Sontag, Susan. *AIDS and Its Metaphors*. New York: Farrar, Straus and Giroux, 1989.
Stravinsky, Igor. *The Rite of Spring*. Choreography by Vaslav Nijinsky. First performed by the Ballets Russes, Théâtre des Champs-Élysées, Paris, May 29, 1913.
Tarkovsky, Andrei, dir. *Stalker*. Moscow: Goskino, 1979.
Tarr, Béla, and Ágnes Hranitzky, dirs. *The Turin Horse*. Budapest: Másképp Alapítvány, 2011.
Teilhard de Chardin, Pierre. "The Mass on the World." In *Hymn of the Universe*, translated by Simon Bartholomew, 1–23. New York: Harper & Row, 1965.
Trier, Lars von, dir. *Breaking the Waves*. Beverly Hills: October, 1996.
———, dir. *Dancer in the Dark*. Burbank: Fine Line, 2000.
———, dir. *Dogville*. Copenhagen: Nordisk, 2003.
Valente, José Ángel. *Fragmentos de un libro futuro*. Barcelona: Galaxia Gutenberg, 2000.
Velázquez, Diego. *Las meninas*. 1656. Oil on canvas. Museo del Prado, Madrid.
Vuong, Ocean. *On Earth We're Briefly Gorgeous: A Novel*. New York: Penguin, 2019.
Weil, Simone. *Gravity and Grace*. Translated by Emma Crawford and Mario von der Ruhr. Routledge Classics. London: Routledge, 2002.
Williams, Rowan. *On Christian Theology*. Oxford: Blackwell, 2000.
Wiman, Christian. *My Bright Abyss: Meditation of a Modern Believer*. New York: Farrar, Straus and Giroux, 2013.
Wright, N. T. *The Resurrection of the Son of God*. Vol. 3 of *Christian Origins and the Question of God*. Minneapolis: Fortress, 2003.

BIBLIOGRAPHY

Zahn, Gordon. *In Solitary Witness: The Life and Death of Franz Jägerstätter*. Springfield, IL: Templegate, 1986.

Žižek, Slavoj. "The Fear of Four Words: A Modest Plea for the Hegelian Reading of Christianity." In *The Monstrosity of Christ: Paradox or Dialectic?*, by Slavoj Žižek and John Milbank, edited by Creston Davis, 24–109. Short Circuits. Cambridge, MA: MIT Press, 2009.

———. *Living in the End Times*. Essential Žižek. London: Verso, 2010.

———. *On Belief*. Thinking in Action. London: Routledge, 2001.

———. *The Puppet and the Dwarf: The Perverse Core of Christianity*. Short Circuits. Cambridge, MA: MIT Press, 2003.

Zumthor, Peter. *Bruder Klaus Field Chapel*. 2007. Architecture. Wachendorf, Mechernich, Germany.

www.ingramcontent.com/pod-product-compliance
Lightning Source LLC
Chambersburg PA
CBHW020855160426
43192CB00007B/931